Also from Westphalia Press
westphaliapress.org

Issues in Maritime Cyber Security

International or Local Ownership?: Security Sector Development in Post-Independent Kosovo

Energy Law and Policy in a Climate-Constrained World

The Role of Theory in Policy Analysis

ABC of Criminology

Non-Profit Organizations and Disaster

The Zelensky Method

Donald J. Trump's Presidency: International Perspectives

Masonic Myths and Legends

Ukraine vs. Russia: Revolution, Democracy and War: Selected Articles and Blogs, 2010-2016

Iran: Who Is Really In Charge?

Stamped: An Anti-Travel Novel

A Strategy for Implementing the Reconciliation Process

The Idea of the Digital University

Dialogue in the Roman-Greco World

The Politics of Impeachment

Discourse of the Inquisitive

The Limits of Moderation: Jimmy Carter and the Ironies of American Liberalism

Frontline Diplomacy: A Memoir of a Foreign Service Officer in the Middle East

Unworkable Conservatism: Small Government, Freemarkets, and Impracticality

Springfield: The Novel

Abortion and Informed Common Sense

Ongoing Issues in Georgian Policy and Public Administration

Growing Inequality: Bridging Complex Systems, Population Health and Health Disparities

The Lord of the Desert: A Study of the Papers of the British Officer John B. Glubb in Jordan and Iraq

The Politics of Fiscal Responsibility: A Comparative Perspective

Pacific Hurtgen: The American Army in Northern Luzon, 1945

New Frontiers in Criminology

Feeding the Global South

Demand the Impossible: Essays in History as Activism

A Different Dimension: Reflections on the History of Transpersonal Thought

The Story of Panama: The New Route to India

The Story of Panama: The New Route to India

All Rights Reserved © 2023 by Policy Studies Organization

Westphalia Press
An imprint of Policy Studies Organization
1527 New Hampshire Ave., NW
Washington, D.C. 20036
info@ipsonet.org

ISBN-13: 978-1-63723-633-8

Cover design by Jeffrey Barnes:
jbarnesbook.design

Daniel Gutierrez-Sandoval, Executive Director
PSO and Westphalia Press

Updated material and comments on this edition
can be found at the Westphalia Press website:
www.westphaliapress.org

The Story of Panama: The New Route to India

by Frank A. Gause and Charles Carr

WESTPHALIA PRESS
An imprint of
Policy Studies Organization

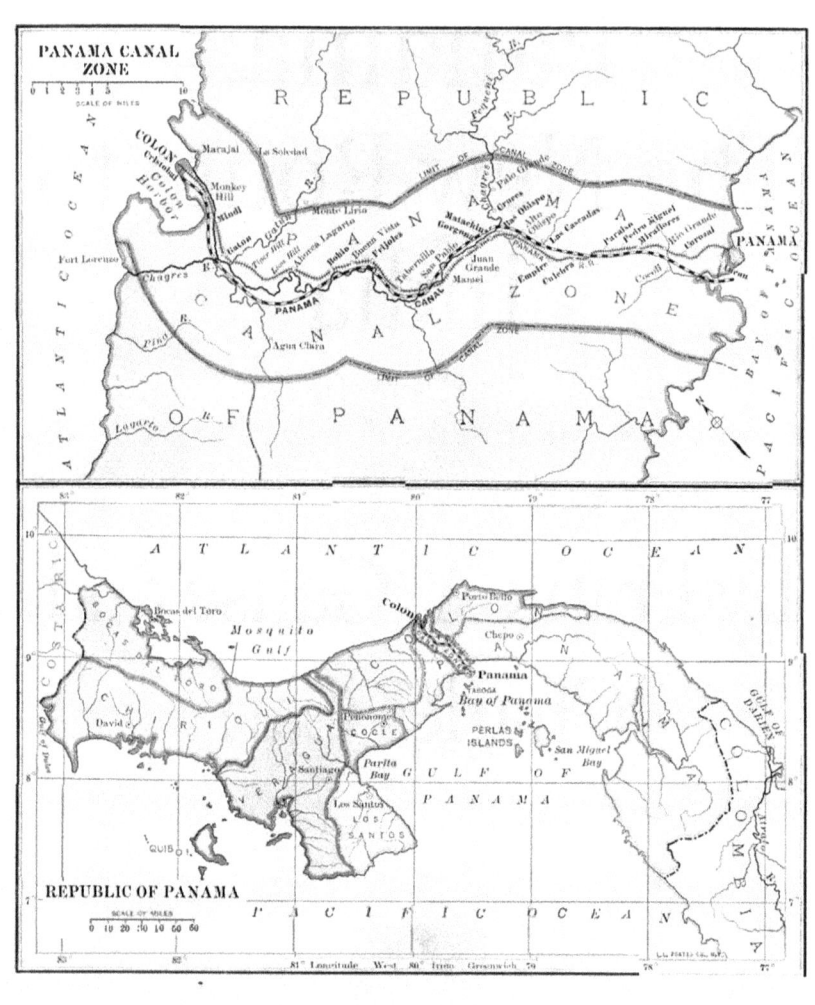

THE STORY OF PANAMA

THE NEW ROUTE TO INDIA

BY

FRANK A. GAUSE

SUPERINTENDENT CANAL ZONE PUBLIC SCHOOLS

AND

CHARLES CARL CARR

PRINCIPAL CANAL ZONE PUBLIC HIGH SCHOOL

SILVER, BURDETT AND COMPANY

BOSTON   NEW YORK   CHICAGO

COPYRIGHT, 1912,
BY SILVER, BURDETT AND COMPANY

PREFACE

THE attention of the world is now turned upon Panama. For Panama that is no new experience. American history had its beginnings in this part of the world. From the day when Columbus found his path to the Indies obstructed by the low-lying Isthmus, a shorter route to India has been the dream of men and of nations.

So the story of Panama involves an account of great exploits and of great achievements. There were the daring explorers and the hardy buccaneers; then the stirring days of canal making, with Panama as the scene of the greatest engineering feat of modern times; and already there are evidences of coming expansion in new directions, following the operation of the canal.

Yet this great canal only represents improved facilities for handling a long-established transisthmian traffic. There were trade routes and trade centers on the Isthmus of Panama half a century before the foundations of St. Augustine were laid, and a century before the first permanent English colony in North America was established at Jamestown. If present plans materialize, the Isthmian canal will be dedicated to the world's commerce on the four hundredth anniversary of the establishment of the old Royal Road, the first commercial highway across the two Americas.

The story of the canal as an engineering project has already been written in engineering terms, for engineers. Its picturesque features have also been displayed in many forms by writers whose acquaintance with the work and with the country was necessarily limited to the observations of a few days. But there still seems to be place for an account of the principal features of the construction as witnessed during several years' residence in the Canal Zone. Because of the authors' long acquaintance with the country and association with the actual work THE STORY OF PANAMA tells at first hand of life and conditions in Panama; and it is hoped that it will do something toward correcting misapprehensions and arousing new interest.

The authors owe much to the Canal Zone officials and to the officials of the Republic of Panama, who have accorded them every courtesy in the preparation of this book and have given them access to many unusual illustrations.

ANCON, CANAL ZONE,
October 31, 1912.

CONTENTS

PART ONE: CANAL MAKING

CHAPTER		PAGE
I.	The Birth of the Project	1
II.	The French Attempt	7
III.	Panama becomes a Republic	17
IV.	On the Works	30
V.	The Big Cut	78
VI.	Organization	97
VII.	Quartermaster's Department	101
VIII.	Sanitation	111
IX.	Subsistence Department	124
X.	Department of Civil Administration	132
XI.	Other Departments	150

PART TWO: THE CANAL COUNTRY

I.	Columbus	159
II.	Balboa	168
III.	The Royal Road	179
IV.	Sir Francis Drake	196
V.	Morgan's Isthmian Raids	205
VI.	Panama and the Pirates	218
VII.	The Land of Dreams	227
VIII.	The Panama of To-day	243
IX.	The Panama Railroad	258
X.	Diplomacy of Two Hundred and Fifty Years	268

LIST OF ILLUSTRATIONS

PART ONE

	PAGE
MAP OF THE REPUBLIC OF PANAMA, (In color)	
MAP OF THE CANAL ZONE, (In color)	
THE COLUMBUS MONUMENT AT CRISTOBAL	xvi
LANDS THAT COLUMBUS DISCOVERED	5
THE FOUR MOST FAVORABLE ROUTES	5
TOSCANELLI'S MAP OF THE WORLD	5
INTERSECTION OF AMERICAN AND FRENCH CANALS	6
IDLE SINCE THE FRENCH DAYS	11
CULEBRA CUT AS THE FRENCH LEFT IT	11
AN OLD ANCHOR FOUND NEAR CRUCES	15
CULEBRA CUT EXCAVATIONS	16
PESTILENTIAL PANAMA OF FRENCH DAYS	23
TRANSFORMED PANAMA OF AMERICAN DAYS	24
JUST OFF CRISTOBAL	31
ROOSEVELT AVENUE, CRISTOBAL	35
CAMP BIERD, THE WEST INDIAN SECTION OF CRISTOBAL	39
DIAGRAM OF LADDER DREDGE	41
A PAIR OF THE BIG GATES, GATUN LOCKS	45
THE GREAT WATER PIPE IN THE "FILL"	49
LOADING BUCKETS WITH CEMENT, AT GATUN	49
GATUN DAM, SPILLWAY AND LOCKS	51
DIAGRAM OF SPILLWAY	52
"BEFORE"	53

LIST OF ILLUSTRATIONS

	PAGE
"After"	54
Diagram of Cross-section of Locks	58
Monoliths in Middle Wall, Upper Gatun	59
Gatun Upper Locks, showing Gate Sills	59
West Chamber, Gatun Upper Locks	63
Forebay and Lift Sill, Gatun Locks	63
A Typical Labor Train	67
Track shifting Machine	73
Mosquitoes	75
Pay Car at Culebra	79
Culebra Slide, West Bank, looking South	80
Culebra Cut, Cross Section	81
Steam Shovel loading rock, Culebra Cut	83
Bottom of Canal raised through Pressure	84
Culebra Cut from Contractor's Hill	84
A Seagoing Suction Dredge	87
Pedro Miguel Locks, looking South	88
Pedro Miguel Locks, looking North	88
On the Way from Balboa to Ancon	91
Hotel Tivoli	92
The Isthmian Canal Commission	96
Organization Chart	99
Sleeping Quarters for Negroes	105
Labor Quarters	105
A Bedroom in Family Quarters	106
Y. M. C. A. Clubhouse	106
Malaria Chart	113
Applying Larvacide with Knapsack Spray	119
Burning Grass from Sides of a Ditch	119
Entrance to Ancon Hospital Grounds	120

LIST OF ILLUSTRATIONS

	PAGE
I. C. C. Sanitarium at Taboga	120
Meal time at an I. C. C. Kitchen	129
Squad of Canal Zone Mounted Police	139
A Quartermaster's Corral	139
School Garden at Empire	147
Primary Grades at Play, Gatun White School	148
Native School, San Miguel	148

PART TWO

Christopher Columbus	161
Balboa discovering the Pacific Ocean	173
"Morgan's Bridge," entrance to Old Panama	181
A Glimpse of the Royal Road	181
Historic Villages as they are To-day	185
Porto Bello, showing Canal Zone Village	193
Old Porto Bello as it is To-day	194
The Panama Tree	197
Fort Lorenzo of To-day	213
Ruins of a Sentry Box	231
Tower of St. Anastasius	223
San Blas Indians at Armilla	229
Natives pounding Rice	237
Wash Day at Taboga	238
San Blas Indian Woman	241
Chiriqui Volcano and Boquete Valley	247
Native Hotel, David	247
Patio Scene near David	248
Presidential Election Day, David	248
Pearl Islands, Panama Bay	253
Pearl Divers	253

LIST OF ILLUSTRATIONS

	PAGE
THE PANAMA LOTTERY.	253
SKATING ON SEA WALL	253
AT FORT LORENZO	254
IN THE JUNGLE	265
GATHERING COCONUTS	266
A PINEAPPLE PLANTATION	266
CITY OF PANAMA, FROM ANCON HILL	271
THE GOVERNMENT PALACE, PANAMA	272
CATHEDRAL PLAZA, PANAMA	277
INSTALLING THE WATER SYSTEM, PANAMA	277

PART ONE

CANAL MAKING

THE COLUMBUS MONUMENT AT CRISTOBAL

CHAPTER I

THE BIRTH OF THE PROJECT

WHEN Columbus, searching for a new route to the Orient, chanced to land in the West Indies, the natives there told him strange stories about a strait through which one might travel westward into waters that led directly to the land for which he was seeking. His belief in these stories increased as his later voyages took him closer and closer to the western continent and finally to the mainland itself.

In those days maps were based on beliefs as well as on facts. The faith Columbus had in this secret strait which he had never seen is shown in the map that was inspired by him, although not published until two years after his death. This map has no Isthmus of Panama, but shows in its place a strait permitting direct passage from Europe to India.

Following Columbus came Balboa with his exploration of the Isthmus and his discovery of the Pacific Ocean. Curiously enough, the legend of a strait still persisted. The Indians told Balboa that across the newly discovered isthmus there was an all-water connection between the Atlantic Ocean and the "South Sea." Balboa believed this story just as Columbus had believed the legend told him by other Indian tribes.

Geographers and explorers accepted the existence of this unseen strait, and the discovery of the elusive and mysterious stream became the chief incentive to most of the exploration up and down the coast. The explorers never found the strait, but out of their failure grew the idea of digging a waterway to connect the two oceans.

And so the Panama Canal is not a project of the twentieth century; nor yet of the nineteenth. The conception dates back to 1523. The project was first proposed to Charles V of Spain fully two hundred and fifty years before the birth of the nation destined to construct the canal.

It was Hernando Cortez, the Spanish conqueror of Mexico, who first proposed making the great waterway. Cortez was sent by his monarch, Charles V, to find the strait which was said to connect the Atlantic and the Pacific oceans. He searched diligently along the Spanish Main, with an expenditure of much time, energy and money.

Failing to find this mythical stream, the stern old *conquistador* determined upon the brilliant expedient of making a strait. His plans were cut short by the treachery of his followers, but he deserves mention as the pioneer in a movement which men were destined to exploit for four centuries. He encouraged his cousin, Alvaro de Saavedra Ceron, to follow up his work; and Saavedra finally drew plans for four transisthmian water routes, intending to submit these plans to the king of Spain.

The routes which Saavedra had in mind were the four that have received most attention in later years — Darien, Nicaragua, Tehuantepec and Panama; but he did not live long enough to develop any one of these plans. Then Charles V encouraged other explorers to continue the search for a natural water route. It was not until the abdication of Charles V and the accession of Philip II that the Spanish ceased the attempt either to find an all-water passage or to pierce the Isthmus.

Philip II introduced a reactionary policy which put an end to Spanish enterprise along that line for almost a hundred years. After an unfavorable report from Antonelli, who had been sent out by the king to survey the Nicaraguan route, Philip laid the matter before his Dominican friars, who in reply quoted from the Bible, "What God hath joined together, let no man put asunder." Deciding that this passage referred directly to Panama, the Spanish king forbade any further attempts àt canal making as sacrilegious.

From the time that Cortez conceived the idea of *making* a strait to the first attempt at its actual accomplishment, three and a half centuries later, the

Isthmus of Panama was the center of stirring events. The conquest of Peru, the pirate raids of Drake and of Morgan, the diplomatic skirmishes of England and Spain, all contributed to keep Panama in the eye of the world.

The United States had been slow to recognize the commercial necessity for a transisthmian canal, but the subject was frequently considered in Congress during the first half of the nineteenth century. One commissioner after another was sent to investigate possible routes and to approach the states of Central America whose coöperation was essential to any such project. Various plans were made, and at several different times a canal under American control seemed to be assured; but always some insuperable difficulty was encountered.

While canal building was still under discussion, three enterprising Americans built the Panama railroad, which for a time served to relieve the imperative demand for transcontinental transportation. During the late fifties and early sixties the United States was too deeply engrossed with the vital issues of the Civil War to consider canal construction; and before the country was prepared to take the matter up in all earnestness the French were ready to engineer and to finance a canal. This was not, however, their first Isthmian Canal project, for they had previously made several attempts.

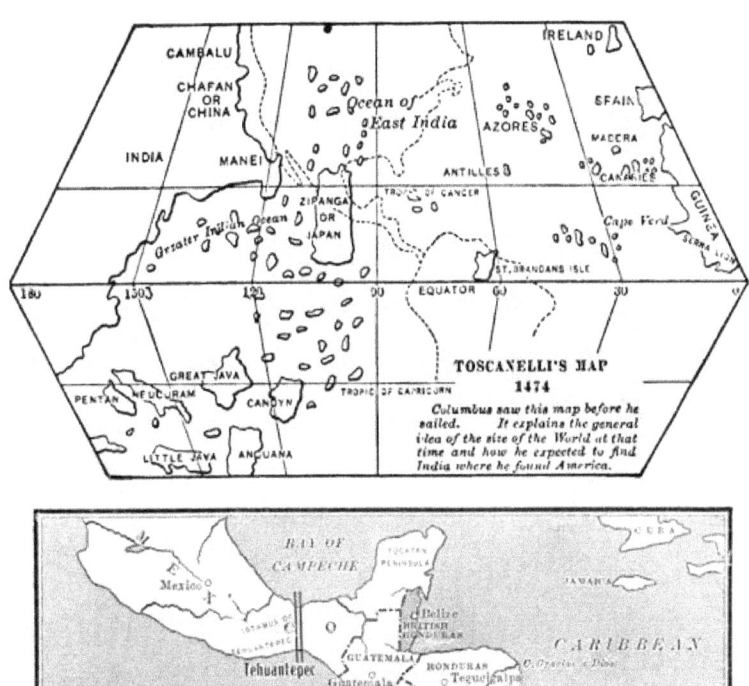

TOSCANELLI'S MAP
1474

Columbus saw this map before he sailed. It explains the general idea of the size of the World at that time and how he expected to find India where he found America.

FOUR MOST FAVORABLE CANAL ROUTES

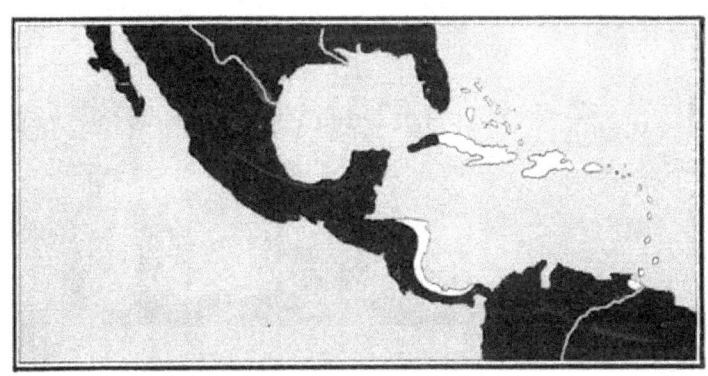

LANDS WHICH COLUMBUS DISCOVERED

INTERSECTION OF AMERICAN AND FRENCH CANALS

CHAPTER II

THE FRENCH ATTEMPT

In March, 1876, at the suggestion of Count Ferdinand de Lesseps, the Society of Commercial Geography at Paris organized a committee to go into the subject of the projected Isthmian Canal. De Lesseps, whose success in engineering the operations at Suez commended him to the Society, was chosen to preside at the deliberations of this body.

The Committee held its first meeting at Paris in May, 1879. It at once took upon itself an international character, as the name under which it worked implied—"The International Scientific Congress." Representatives from nearly all the civilized nations of the world were present. The discussion lasted for several months, but the conclusions of the Committee may be summed up in these words: "The Congress thinks that the construction of an interoceanic waterway on a constant level is possible; that in the interests of commerce and navigation a sea level canal is desirable; that the most practicable route lies between the Gulf of Limon and the Bay of Panama." The Committee believed the cost would approximate $240,000,000.

Here, then, were the three paramount questions: (1) What kind of canal was to be built? (2) What was to be its location? (3) What would it cost? The wisdom of the conclusions of the Committee has been confirmed on only one point, that of location. A sea level canal is now believed to be out of the question, even with present-day machinery and methods. It is estimated that the lock canal will cost $375,000,000, and it is certain that a sea level canal would cost several times that amount, if indeed it could be built at all.

As the plans of De Lesseps had been incorporated in the Committee's report (against the vote of a majority of the engineers on the Committee) and as the Count had demonstrated his ability to build canals, he was given the direction of the project.

On the 17th of August, 1879, a company was organized under the significant title, *Compagnie Universelle du Canal Interoceanique* (The Universal Interoceanic Canal Company). M. de Lesseps' confidence in the success of the project is indicated in an address he made at the time. He said, "If a general who has won his first battle is asked whether he desires the chance to win another, he cannot refuse." While De Lesseps appears to have had no doubt about the successful issue of the undertaking, the project was viewed with misgiving by more deliberate men, many of whom looked upon it at that time as altogether impracticable.

But the romantic nature of the undertaking appealed to the French people, and the eighty million dollars' worth of stock offered for sale was taken within a short time. The enthusiastic De Lesseps, encouraged by the readiness with which this stock was purchased, believed that all was over except a little work and much shouting. However, it is not strange that a man who had just built the Suez Canal — a man endowed with the optimistic temperament of the best blood of France — should declare, "Those who have counted only on a lock canal have committed a serious blunder; a sea level canal is not only the most desirable, but is easily possible."

Prior to the organization of the Interoceanic Canal Company, a French syndicate had secured from Colombia a concession for the construction of a canal. This concession was transferred to the De Lesseps company. The surveys authorized made it necessary that the canal company invade the territory that had previously been ceded to the Panama Railroad Company. This, and the fact that the control of the railroad facilities would be valuable during the construction of the canal, rendered it advisable to take over the stock of the railroad company, which was purchased at a high figure, $18,000,000.

The actual work of digging the canal began in May, 1882. Tracy Robinson thus describes the occasion: "The company was assembled to witness the formal opening of the great work. The Bishop of Panama was to give it his blessing. A tremendous charge of dynamite was to be exploded. . . . An eyewitness has described the scene for us: 'The blessing had been pronounced. There the crowd stood, breathless, ears stopped, eyes blinking, half in terror lest this artificial earthquake might involve general destruction. But there was no explosion! It wouldn't go!'" This is a beginning typical of the long, sad attempt of the French. It simply would not go.

The canal was to be of the sea level type, thirty feet deep and seventy-two feet minimum width at the bottom. The continental divide was to be pierced by a tunnel. This last scheme, however, was soon abandoned and the present open cut substituted for the tunnel.

De Lesseps pushed the work vigorously, but very early in the course of operations there began to arise those serious obstacles foreseen by the trained engineers, who had voted against the great director almost to a man. The floods of the Chagres, disease, distrust — a thousand obstacles unforeseen by the brave Frenchman, crowded upon him to discourage, thwart and finally to overwhelm him.

I. IDLE SINCE THE FRENCH DAYS (11)
II. CULEBRA CUT AS THE FRENCH LEFT IT

The early confidence in De Lesseps' ability to accomplish this great task soon began to wane. Subscriptions for stock dwindled to such an extent that by the middle of the year 1887 it became evident that if the work was to continue there must be a change both in the organization of the company and in the original plan of the canal. De Lesseps relinquished the directorship of the enterprise and returned home to be tried and disgraced in the courts of his native land. Though exonerated of the charge of misappropriation of the funds intrusted to him, he became insane as a result of his failure, and died in 1894, not knowing that his countrymen, grateful for the services he had rendered the world by his achievement at Suez, would one day erect an appropriate monument to his memory on the site of his successes.

In 1887, the sea level type of canal was abandoned for the lock type. But the change came too late, and in 1889 the company went into the hands of a receiver. The story of the French attempt may be summed up in one statement: Eighty million cubic yards of earth had been excavated at a cost of $260,000,000.

When this story is impartially written, it will tell how brave men suffered, despaired, died in an unsuccessful though none the less heroic effort to advance the world's interests. Everywhere along the canal line in the early days of American operations were sad evidences of the French failure. Rusty, broken-down, jungle-covered locomotives, cars, cranes, excavators; stacks of bent, twisted steel rails; sunken dredges, tugs and anchors, marked the path of the French failure from Panama to Colon, and testified to the eyes of the traveler in no unmistakable terms of the serious mindedness of those men who were bold in conception but erring in their estimate of the magnitude of the undertaking.

The diagram on page 16 shows the comparative amounts of excavation accomplished by the French in their seven years' trial and by the Americans in the years up to July, 1909. It gives convincing proof of the seriousness with which the French company attacked the Herculean task. Says Mr. Rousseau, "When we consider the handicaps in the way of unsanitary conditions under which the French worked, we have increased admiration for what they accomplished."

In 1894 Brunet, the receiver of the French company, transferred its rights and property to "The New Panama Canal Company," which prosecuted the work in a desultory sort of way until 1904, when the canal properties were purchased by the American government for $40,000,000.

AN OLD ANCHOR FOUND NEAR CRUCES

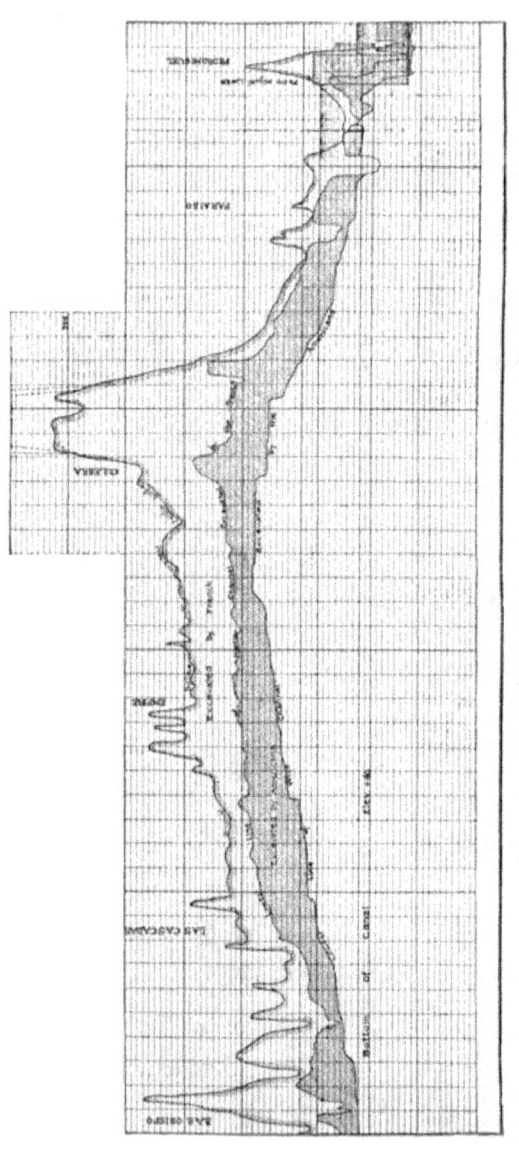

CULEBRA CUT EXCAVATIONS UP TO JUNE 30, 1909

This diagram shows the depth to which the French excavated for a narrow channel; the depth to which the American excavation for the wide channel had been carried to June 30, 1909; and the proposed bottom of the canal.

(16)

CHAPTER III

PANAMA BECOMES A REPUBLIC

THE taking over by the United States of the French properties and concessions was of greater moment in the history of Central American politics than even the wisest statesmen anticipated. The French company held its concession from the United States of Colombia, of which Panama was a dependency. The negotiations incident to American occupation of the canal site precipitated a brief but eventful diplomatic dispute which culminated in the successful revolt of Panama, and in the speedy recognition of her independence by the United States and by the other great powers.

Following the Hay-Pauncefote treaty, which gave the United States the right to build the canal, Congress and the country engaged in a long discussion as to which route should be chosen, Nicaragua or Panama. The Spooner Bill, which finally became a law on June 28, 1902, authorized the President to offer the French company at Panama $40,000,000 for its rights, provided that the government of the United States could also acquire from Colombia, on reasonable terms, a strip of territory for a canal zone. Should the Administration be unable to accomplish this, after waiting a reasonable time for action by Colombia, it was to open negotiations with Nicaragua for a canal route.

Despite the favor with which Americans looked on Panama, it was very soon evident that the Republic of Colombia had little disposition to make what the United States deemed a reasonable treaty. Civil war was in progress in Colombia and had extended to the Isthmus of Panama — that very part of her possessions through which the government of the United States desired a canal zone.

Despite the very favorable terms of the preliminary protocol, in which Colombia was offered a bonus of $7,000,000 and an annuity of $250,000 after fourteen years, that country informed the Secretary of State, John Hay, that she would not accept the proposition. The capital, Bogota, was at that time controlled by politicians who were prone to consider only the immediate future, and were willing to sacrifice the vital interests of Panama, if necessary to secure their ends. The Colombian government claimed that the French company's franchise could only last, at the utmost, until October, 1910, while the Colombian Congress had never ratified its extension beyond 1904. Now if the politicians at Bogota could force Colombia to "sit tight" for a year and a half, until 1904, possibly the

$40,000,000 that the United States was to pay the French company would go, not to that concern, but into the Colombian treasury.

Then Concha, the Colombian Minister, was replaced by Dr. Herran; and on January 22, 1903, the Hay-Herran treaty was drawn up. Under its terms, Colombia was to authorize the French company to sell its property to the United States, to give the United States a strip thirty miles wide for a canal zone, to retain sovereignty over this strip but to give the United States police control. In return Colombia was to get $10,000,000 at once and $100,000 yearly after the ninth year. This treaty the Colombian Congress failed to ratify, and on October 31, 1903, negotiations were finally given up. The Panama proposition looked hopeless unless something speedily happened.

Something did happen. On November 3, 1903, Panama revolted and severed a connection of eighty-two years with the South American republic. Before discussing the incidents of this momentous change let us examine, briefly, the history of Panama as a province of the Republic of Colombia.

When in 1819 that part of South America known as New Granada revolted from Spain under the patriot Simon Bolivar, it was soon joined by Panama, which threw off the Spanish yoke in 1821. This union proved irksome for Panama. Much of the time it was nothing more than a province of Colombia, which did not hesitate to exploit it for her own advantage. After repeated revolutions on the part of the citizens of Panama, Colombia in 1858 formed the *Confederación Granadina,* by which Panama was made one of several "states," self-governing as to internal affairs. This autonomy proved a shadow and was followed in two years by another revolution. Again in 1884 followed still another revolution, resulting in the formation by Colombia of a highly centralized state. From this time on, as one writer expresses it, Panama was the "milch cow for a coterie of politicians at Bogota."

The government at Bogota was never able to maintain effective local government on the Isthmus. One disturbance after another followed in rapid succession through the years. In fifty-seven years there had been fifty-three uprisings. Six times United States marines had landed to protect the property of the Panama Railroad, four times Colombia had requested the United States to protect her Isthmian interests and restore order. The memorable Night of Horror in 1855, when sixteen American lives were lost in a pitched battle at the railroad station in Panama, is an example. Colombia finally paid the American interests $100,000 for property destroyed in this riot.

Let the people of Panama relate a few of their

grievances against Colombia as they have left them in enduring form in their Declaration of Independence: ". . . the people (of Panama) and the Isthmian territory were a source of fiscal revenue to Colombia and nothing more. The contracts and the negotiations of the railroad and the canal in Panama and the national revenues collected on the Isthmus have produced for Colombia immense sums . . .; and from this immense total the Isthmus has not received the benefit of a bridge for any of its many rivers, nor that of the construction of a road between its towns, nor that of a public building, nor that of a school, nor of any interest in promoting any of its industries, nor has the least part of that vast sum been employed in promoting its prosperity." Now on top of these grievances the Isthmian people saw Colombia willing to sacrifice the whole future of Panama by risking the transfer of the canal route to Nicaragua!

That the citizens of Panama did not break away from Colombia with rankling hatred is evidenced by the closing words of their declaration: "In separating ourselves from our brothers of Colombia, we do it without rancor and without joy. As a child that separates itself from the paternal home, the Isthmian people, in adopting the life they have chosen, have done it with sorrow, but in the accomplishment of their supreme and imperious duty. . . .

Let us commence, then, to form ourselves among the free nations of the world, considering Colombia as a sister nation, with whom we shall always be what the circumstances demand and for whose prosperity we have the most fervent and sincere wishes."

In this *résumé* of the revolution itself the names of the many illustrious Panamanian citizens who accomplished it are omitted, because of limited space. Colombia must have known that there existed a revolutionary junta composed of the best citizens of Panama. Indeed, she had not been without warning from the Panamanians themselves that, should she fail to ratify the canal treaty, Panama would declare her independence. Unable to effect the change alone, the Panama junta sought outside aid by sending Dr. Amador to the United States.

This distinguished Panamanian could secure no promises of help from the Washington government. However, he soon saw a way in which that government could be so placed that it would be under the necessity of helping to defend the independence of Panama. If Panama could, by a sudden *coup*, break away from Colombia and declare her independence, then the United States would, perforce, protect its property in Panama from any alien, even if that alien were Colombia itself. With this plan worked out, Dr. Amador returned to Panama. He

PESTILENTIAL PANAMA OF THE FRENCH DAYS

TRANSFORMED PANAMA OF AMERICAN DAYS

(24)

had the support of Philippe Bunau-Varilla, a prominent French engineer, who had his heart set on seeing the Panama Canal built by the United States.

Bunau-Varilla lent his aid to the revolutionary junta, and was selected by it to represent Panama in framing a canal treaty with the United States. Upon Amador's return the wheels of revolution were set in motion.

November 4, 1903, was set for the date of the *coup*, but it was precipitated a day earlier by Colombia herself. Alarmed at last, the government at Bogota sent an "army" to Panama. This army, which was representative of the disorganized condition of Colombia at the time, consisted of four hundred and fifty soldiers. They arrived in Colon, but found that the Panama Railroad would not transport them without carfare — a thing they did not have. The fifteen officers succeeded in getting together the price of transportation to Panama City; they had to leave their forces bivouacked in the streets of Colon.

The officers were met with all courtesy by General Huertas, a Panamanian patriot, who was heart and soul in the revolutionary movement. They were entertained at dinner, but when they asked to see the sea wall they were arrested by General Huertas, at a prearranged signal, and were informed that they were prisoners of war; Panama was independent.

Protestation availing nothing, the Colombians could get out of their plight only by acquiescing gracefully. Meanwhile their soldiers in Colon were being looked after by the citizens and by the Panama Railroad; they were prevented from doing any damage. Five days later the whole Colombian force departed from the Isthmus.

The revolution, effected in a day, was practically bloodless — the only life lost was that of a Chinese coolie who was killed in Panama when one of the three Colombian gunboats fired its only shot into the city. The other two boats raised the Panamanian flag. The local officers of Colombia were arrested as a matter of form; but most of them, like Governor Obaldia, were glad to enroll themselves later as citizens of Panama.

On November 4, Panama was declared a free and independent republic, and on November 7 the United States recognized the Provisional Government. By January, 1904, practically all the nations of the world had recognized the independence of Panama.

Within three months from the date of its Declaration of Independence, Panama had become a self-governing Republic. A constitution was drawn up, and by February 13, 1904, it had been signed by the deputies to the Constitutional Convention and by nearly all the leading Panamanians. The Republic is centralized in form, though the municipal districts in the various provinces have almost unlimited powers of local government. The executive power is vested in the president, elected for four years, with the power of appointing not only his own cabinet, but also the governors of the different provinces. His executive orders, however, must be countersigned by the secretary of state in the particular department to which the order applies. He must be a Panamanian by birth and at least thirty-five years of age. He has a limited veto in legislative matters.

The National Assembly consists of one chamber to which deputies are elected for a term of four years, one deputy for every 10,000 inhabitants. The deputy must be over twenty-five years old and a citizen. The Assembly meets every other year, opening on September first; there may be special sessions. The Supreme Court is composed of five members who must be over thirty years old and must have practiced law for ten years. For the administration of local government there are the municipal districts in the seven provinces of Bocas del Toro, Cocle, Colon, Chiriqui, Los Santos, Panama and Veraguas. There is no state church, but the Republic has subsidized the Roman Catholic Church.

From the first there have been two political parties in the Republic, Liberal and Conservative, the same names as those applied to the parties which existed in Panama when it was a province of Colombia. The national flag represents the friendly rivalry of these parties. It is composed of four fields, one of red and one of blue, alternating with two white fields. The red is for the Liberals, the blue for the Conservatives, while the white fields are for peace.

The most important diplomatic matter in which the new Republic engaged was the consummation of the Hay-Bunau-Varilla treaty which was signed at Washington on November 18, 1903, and proclaimed February 26, 1904. Its terms are, briefly: —

First, the United States guarantees to maintain the independence of the Republic of Panama.

Second, Panama grants to the United States in perpetuity a strip across the Isthmus extending five miles on each side of the canal, the cities of Colon and Panama excepted. Over this strip, called the Canal Zone, the United States is conceded absolute jurisdiction.

Third, all railway and canal rights of the Zone are ceded to the United States.

Fourth, the property of the United States in the Zone is exempt from taxation.

Fifth, the United States is to have the right to use military force, to build fortifications and to perfect transit.

Sixth, the United States is to have sanitary jurisdiction over the cities of Panama and Colon, and the right to preserve order in the Republic should the Panamanian government, in the judgment of the United States, fail to do so.

Seventh, the United States agrees to pay Panama $10,000,000 at once, and to pay an annuity of $250,000, beginning with the year 1913.

CHAPTER IV

ON THE WORKS

THE negotiations which gave us the Canal Zone were not consummated with more despatch and effectiveness than was the work of organizing the forces to construct the canal. The treaty with Panama was ratified in February, 1904, and from that day the work went rapidly forward. To appreciate the magnitude of the task and the effectiveness with which the American organization went at it, let us take a trip to the Canal Zone. For the sake of seeing things as they looked at the most interesting stage in the progress of the work and just as the waters of Gatun Lake began to rise, we will suppose that the time of our visit is back in the year 1911.

We will start from New York. On the evening of the third day out we sight Watling's Island, the first land seen in the New World by Christopher Columbus. We cross the path of the Great Navigator, and on the fourth day round the eastern point of the "Queen of the Antilles." Just as the sun sinks into the Caribbean we see against the eastern sky the blue mountain ranges of Haiti and San Domingo;

JUST OFF CRISTOBAL

on the morning of the sixth day out the captain who has been scanning the horizon announces that the end of our journey is in sight.

That scene is one not soon to be forgotten. As the sun bursts through the clouds hanging over "Fair Marguerita's Hill" the whole world seems lit up with the glory that Keats describes as "wild and celestial." The time and place are full of sentiment. Upon those same hills the great Columbus looked four centuries ago; over these same trackless waters glided the swift craft of the buccaneers, laden with booty; and

> "The waves are softly murmuring
> Stories of the days of old."

Far to the east of the low-lying, palm-bedecked island of Manzanillo are the blue foothills of the Cordilleras, just awakening from their heavy sleep; away to the south stretches the valley of the Chagres; while there beyond Toro's palms Lorenzo rises out of the sea

> "Guarding the Chagres' entrance still."

The *cayucas* and sailboats in the harbor belong to San Blas Indians, who have come from down the coast forty or fifty miles, with coconuts, bananas, beads, beautifully woven textiles and other products. They have brought their children with them. The voyage, in fact, has been a part of the manual training of the youngsters, and the bartering done by their parents has been a lesson in business methods which they must some day apply. Measured by the standards of the society in which these children are to move as men, there will be no failures.

To the east, to the west, to the south are primeval jungles, still the habitations of primitive men and savage beasts — undisturbed by the vandalism of civilization. After passing the artificial land extension which is to form the breakwater for the Atlantic entrance to the canal, and which, by the way, is the first evidence of the work of the canal builders, we come into Limon Bay, just off the twin cities of Colon and Cristobal. Soon we have a full view of the beautiful Cristobal, whose harbor we are about to enter. Our reveries are suddenly interrupted by the command to "assemble in the saloon." The Quarantine Officer is coming aboard. His work done, we land.

After inspection we are allowed to pass the ropes. The train standing there at our dock is a "special" waiting to take recruits for the service or those returning from leave. Passing out at the north end of Pier 11 we come in full view of the old De Lesseps buildings, now used for offices by the Commissary, Subsistence and other departments.

We pass out upon Roosevelt Avenue and then

ROOSEVELT AVENUE, CRISTOBAL.

get a first glimpse of the quarters furnished white employees. They are not unlike the commodious quarters to be seen everywhere along the canal line. They are the homes of Americans who, because they are happy and contented, are bringing to a speedy conclusion this greatest of human undertakings. But if we are to see the canal in a day, we must hurry. As we are bound for Gatun, we will take a cab and drive to the pier. How clean the paved streets are! Passing the post office, the police station, the Y. M. C. A. clubhouse, the I. C. C. hotel, the white school building and the fire station, we come out through the West Indian section of Cristobal to Pier 13. That boat at the wharf is a dynamite carrier, and the men are just beginning to unload one and one quarter million pounds of dynamite for use in blasting. This load of dynamite is a part of the twelve million pounds brought annually from New York.

The boat unloading there to those sand cars has carried sand down from Nombre de Dios for the concrete construction at Gatun. The forty or fifty other large and small vessels you see plying in the bay are the dredges and tugs in the service of the Atlantic Division of the Department of Construction and Engineering; and there is a boat with rock from the quarries at Porto Bello, twenty miles down the coast. This sand and rock will become a part of the two million cubic yards of concrete to be molded into the great locks at Gatun.

Just below us are the docks, and the huge buildings you see beyond are those of the Mount Hope storehouse — the clearing house for all the departments on the canal. In them are stored stationery, school supplies, desks, nails, wire, steel rods, rope, chain, household furniture, steam shovels, tools and equipment of every description. There is a stock here at all times averaging about $4,000,000 worth of material. As needed, this material is requisitioned through the heads of departments and is shipped by rail to the points where it is to be used. The place is in charge of the Depot Quartermaster.

But time is passing. To the left of us is Mount Hope cemetery. It is not difficult to imagine that the place took its name from the feeling back in the French days that this was the one hope to which the ill-fed, ill-quartered, fever-stricken employees could look with any degree of satisfaction — Mount Hope, indeed!

From Pier 13 we may take a boat for Gatun. We pass first into the mouth of the old French canal. The intent of its original builders was to make it thirty feet deep and seventy feet wide at the bottom. For four miles we pass up the channel of the French canal, which crosses the line of the American canal at Mindi. The sunken boats and dredges which

CAMP BIERD, THE WEST INDIAN SECTION OF CRISTOBAL

(39)

we see on both sides were at one time considered the best excavating machines in the world. Left to combat rain, sun and the sea, they at last yielded to their fate and lie there at the bottom of the watery grave they themselves helped to dig. These machines represent another source of enormous loss to the French company. Some of them survive and are

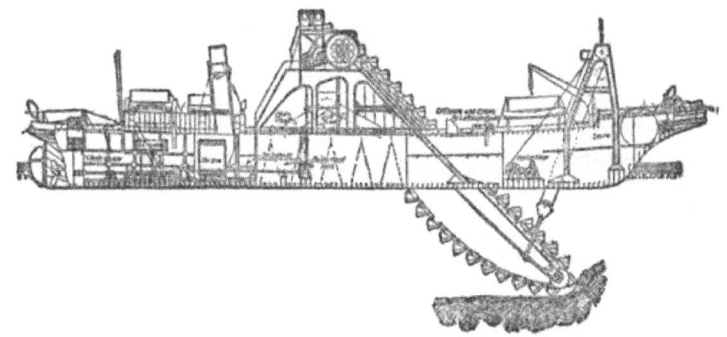

DIAGRAM OF A LADDER DREDGE

now doing good work for the Isthmian Canal Commission. The ladder dredge you see at work is one of the survivors.

When we come to Mindi we find, running to right and left at an angle of about forty-five degrees, the channel of the American canal. At this point the old and the new canals intersect, to converge again in the Chagres River at Gatun. To get to grade at this point nearly forty feet of solid rock blasting had to be done. Imagine the expense of constructing a sea level canal when here, within sight of the sea, and yet thirty miles from the continental divide, it becomes necessary to excavate through solid rock for a depth of more than forty feet!

While we are approaching the great dam, we might gather some general information. The frontispiece map indicates the extent of the Canal Zone, the line of the Canal and the Zone boundaries, and the location of Gatun Lake, formed from the impounding of the Chagres by Gatun Dam.

In a booklet compiled by Mr. Joseph Bucklin Bishop, Secretary of the Commission, there is a condensed table, which summarizes the canal statistics; revised to October 1, 1912, they are: —

Canal Statistics

Length from deep water to deep water (miles)	50
Length from shore line to shore line (miles)	40
Bottom width of channel, maximum (feet)	1000
Bottom width of channel, minimum, 9 miles, Culebra Cut (feet)	300
Locks, in pairs	12
Locks, usable length (feet)	1000
Locks, usable width (feet)	110
Gatun Lake, area (square miles)	164
Gatun Lake, channel depth (feet)	85 to 45
Culebra Cut, channel depth (feet)	45
Excavation, estimated total (cubic yards)	200,000,000

Excavation, amount accomplished October 1, 1912 (cubic yards)	180,000,000
Excavation by the French (cubic yards) .	78,146,960
Excavation by French, useful to present Canal (cubic yards)	29,908,000
Excavation by French, estimated value to Canal	$25,389,240
Value of all French property	$42,799,826
Concrete, total estimated for Canal (cubic yards)	5,000,000
Time of transit through completed Canal (hours)	10 to 12
Time of passage through locks (hours) . .	3
Relocated Panama Railroad, estimated cost	$9,000,000
Relocated Panama Railroad, length (miles)	47.1
Canal Zone, area (square miles)	448
Canal and Panama Railroad force actually at work (about)	35,000
Canal and Panama Railroad force, Americans (about)	5000
Cost of Canal, estimated total	$375,000,000
Work begun by Americans	May 4, 1904
Anticipated date of completion	Jan. 1, 1915

In an article in the *National Geographic Magazine* of February, 1911, Colonel Goethals gives the following condensed statement: —

"The canal which is now building consists of a sea level entrance channel from the sea through Limon Bay to Gatun, about 7 miles long, 500 feet bottom width, and 41 feet deep at mean tide. At Gatun the 85-foot lake level is obtained by a dam across the valley. The lake is confined on the Pacific side by a dam between the hills at Pedro Miguel, 32 miles away. The lake thus formed will have an area of 164 square miles and a channel depth of not less than 45 feet at normal stage.

"At Gatun ships will pass from the sea to the lake level, and *vice versa*, by three locks in flight. On the Pacific side there will be one lift of 30 feet at Pedro Miguel to a small lake held at 55 feet above sea level by dams at Miraflores, where two lifts overcome the difference of level to the sea. The channel between the locks on the Pacific side will be 500 feet wide at the bottom and 45 feet deep, and below the Miraflores locks the sea level section, about 8 miles in length, will be 500 feet wide at the bottom and 45 feet deep at mean tide. Through the lake the bottom widths are not less than 1000 feet for about 16 miles, 800 feet for about 4 miles, 500 feet for about 3 miles, and through the continental divide, a distance of about 9 miles, the bottom width is 300 feet.

"The total length of the canal from deep water in the Caribbean, 41-foot depth at mean tide, to deep water in the Pacific, 45-foot depth at mean tide, is practically 50 miles, 15 miles of which are at sea level. The variation in tide on the Atlantic side is 2.5 feet as a maximum, and on the Pacific it is 21.1 feet as a maximum.

"Provisions are made to amply protect the entrances of the canal. During the winter months occasional storms occur on the Atlantic side of such violence that vessels cannot lie with safety in Colon Harbor, and during

A PAIR OF THE BIG GATES, GATUN LOCKS

(45)

the progress of such storms entrance and egress from the canal would be unsafe. To overcome this condition, a breakwater will extend out about two miles from Toro Point in a northeasterly direction, which will not only protect the entrance, but will provide a safe harbor.

"The Pacific entrance requires no protection from storms, but the set of the silt-bearing current from the east is at right angles to the channel, and the silting made constant dredging necessary. To prevent this shoaling a dike is being constructed from the mainland at Balboa to Naos Island, a distance of about four miles."

The following table presents comparative data: —

Great Canals	Kind	When Opened to Commerce	Length in Miles	Cost	Connects
Erie	Lock	1825	363	$8,000,000[1]	Lake Erie and Hudson River
Soo	Lock	1855	1.5	10,000,000	Lakes Superior and Huron
Suez	Sea level	1869	90	100,000,000	Mediterranean and Red Seas
Kronstadt . .	Sea level	1890	16	10,000,000	St. Petersburg and Bay of Kronstadt
Corinth . . .	Sea level	1893	4	5,000,000	Gulfs of Corinth and Ægina
Manchester .	Lock	1894	35	75,000,000	Liverpool and Manchester
Kaiser Wilhelm	Lock	1895	60	40,000,000	Niemen River and the Baltic
Elbe-Trave . .	Lock	1900	41	6,000,000	Elbe and Trave
Panama . . .	Lock	1915	50	375,000,000	Atlantic and Pacific Oceans

[1] Original cost.

While the great dam is still half a mile away we may get a good conception of its general plan. To the extreme left are massive walls of concrete. These are the walls of the locks. The mound of earth to the right is the dam proper, which is pierced near the middle by the spillway. It may be said that the construction of the Panama Canal involves at once the greatest piece of constructive work and the greatest piece of destructive work ever undertaken by man — the locks, dams and spillways, and the Culebra Cut.

Gatun Dam is about 7500 feet long, 2100 feet wide at the base and 100 feet wide at the summit of the crest, 115 feet above sea level. In building this mountain of earth a huge artificial valley was left in the middle, which is being filled with a mixture of sand and clay pumped in by dredges at work in the vicinity of the dam. The silt settles down into a hard, rock-like mass which is impervious to water. The walls or outer portions of the dam are built from dry excavation brought in from other points along the canal.

Our boat lands at the foot of the dam. Let us climb the man-made mountain. There, right before us, is the great water pipe pouring forth its black slime into what is to be the core of the dam. This sea of mud the engineers term the hydraulic fill. The other end of the pipe connects with a suction

I. THE GREAT WATER PIPE IN THE "FILL" (49)
II. LOADING BUCKETS WITH CEMENT, AT GATUN

dredge nearly a mile distant. The excavation, wet and dry, used in the construction of the dam aggregates 21,000,000 cubic yards.

Below is a diagram of the entire work. We are standing at the point marked X, facing to the southeast. To the left are the great locks. In front of us is the hydraulic fill; to the right, the spillway,

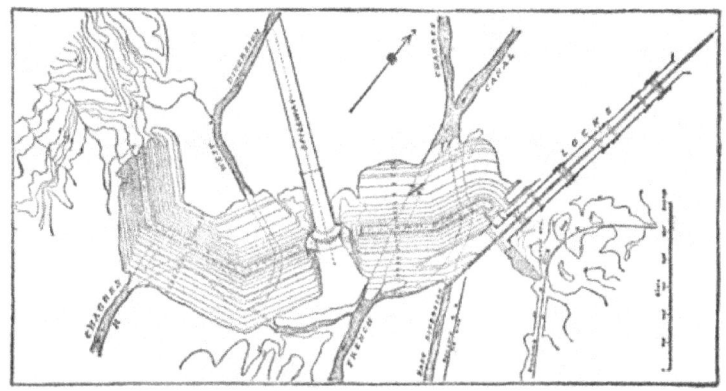

GATUN DAM, SPILLWAY AND LOCKS

with its mad, irresistible torrent of water. Close your eyes, and imagine, if you can, a cement-lined, waterless depression 300 feet wide, 1200 feet long, with forty or fifty huge cubical concrete blocks dispersed at regular intervals near the upper end, the bottom sloping upward from these to the concrete dam, and you have the spillway as it appeared on the day before the Chagres was turned into its new concrete bed. Open your eyes upon the foaming, raging, seething rapids, and you have the contrast presented in the two pictures "Before" and "After." At the foot of the slope the channel of the overflow suddenly widens to twice its previous width. This sudden widening, and the concrete blocks above mentioned, provide two very effective checks to the velocity of the current. These checks are necessary, for without them the under suction which would be

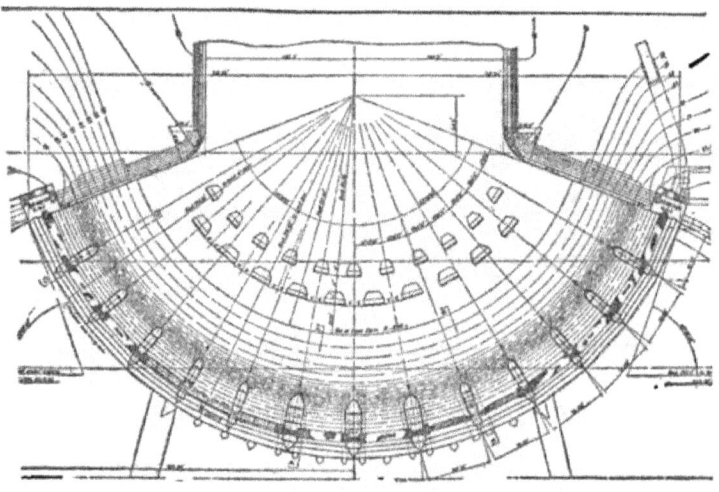

DIAGRAM OF SPILLWAY

caused as the waters leave the concrete floor would quickly undermine the floor itself.

Notice the semicircular construction, made of concrete, that is placed at the head of the spillway. Against this form the spillway dam is being built. At the top of this dam sliding gates will be constructed. From above, the form presents an appearance something like the diagram.

"BEFORE"

(53)

"AFTER"

(54)

By this device the waters of the lake may be raised or lowered when reports from the Alhajuela fluviograph station warn of floods, or when the approaching dry season renders advisable a greater storage supply. The maximum overflow at the spillway may thus always be kept within safe limits, while storage for the dry season may likewise be provided.

Remember, while we walk the next mile, that we are still walking on the dam. An artificial mountain, indeed! Ribboned everywhere with railroad tracks, over which scores of trains run daily, carrying their mites to contribute to the ever growing dam. We again pass around the north side of the hydraulic fill, and approach the factories where the composition that is to go into the locks and into the dam is made.

A most interesting feature is the making, handling and placing of the concrete. The machines with the funnel-shaped nozzles are the concrete mixers. (See second cut, page 49.) The cars standing at the side are run by the third-rail system, so have a care. One of the mixers is now tilted and is filling the bucket with concrete. In a very few minutes all the buckets will be filled, and the little cars will go spinning down the track with their loads of sand, water, stone and cement. We shall see later how this material is deposited in the huge molds in which the locks are being cast. There are four of the big mixers on each side of the shed. We will now walk over to the great concrete locks, where we can see one of them in process of construction. Note the middle wall rising to a height of ninety feet, between the east and west chambers of the locks. (See page 63.) The great cylinder at the base of this wall is one of the three delivery and drainage culverts. This, as you will note, is duplicated in size by culverts in the side walls. The three culverts are eighteen feet minimum diameter and extend the entire length of the walls, or more than three thousand feet.

Above the side walls to the right are the buckets which come from the concrete mixers we visited. These buckets, with their tons of concrete, are hoisted to wire cables attached to steel derricks on either side of the works, and run out on pulleys to the point where the concrete is to be used. They are then lowered, their contents is dumped, and spread by hand. The whole process of delivery involves the labor of a very few men. A daily average of more than twenty-four hundred cubic yards of concrete is thus laid.

A glance at the railroad tracks, regular width, running up into the chambers on either side of the middle wall, will indicate to some extent the proportions of the structure.

The view of the monolith on page 59 shows the culvert with a projecting steel tube. This tube is removed and replaced for another length when the concrete about it becomes set. The steel framework against the left side of the middle wall is supporting a part of the mold into which the concrete form has been cast.

Looking from the east wall one gets a good view of the upper locks, the concrete gate sills, and in the distance the waters of the Chagres backed up by the elevation of the spillway. The lake will rise almost to the elevation of the wall when the dam is completed.

Again, one gets a fair conception of the proportions of this work by a glance at the opening through the gate sills. Through this opening a railway locomotive may pass. Over these gate sills will swing the heavy steel gates. Had you visited the place in March, 1910, you would have seen the foundation work of this mountain of concrete as reproduced on page 63.

The general plan of the locks and their operation is shown in the cross section diagram, page 58. The inside surfaces of the side walls are perpendicular, while the outside surface rises by steps. At the base these walls are fifty feet thick; at the top, eight feet thick. The 'middle wall is slightly more than sixty feet thick. As already indicated, the openings at the base of the walls are for delivery and drainage. The culverts are eighteen feet in diameter, and connect by lateral culverts with openings in the floor,

F F F F. The second chamber in the middle wall, marked *C* in the cut, is the drainage gallery; the third, *B*, will be used for the electrical connections, while the upper chamber, *A*, will furnish working space for the operators of the machinery used in

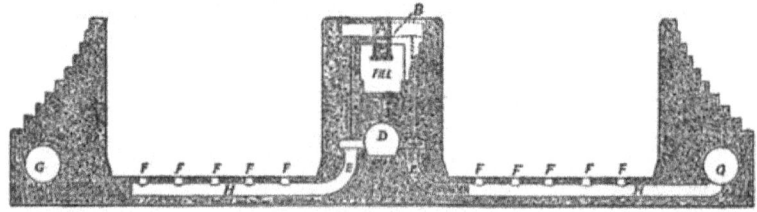

CROSS SECTION OF LOCK CHAMBER AND WALLS

A. — Passageway for operators.
B. — Gallery for electric wires.
C. — Drainage gallery.
D. — Culvert in center wall.
E. — Culverts under the lock floor alternating with those from side walls.
F. — Wells opening from lateral culverts into lock chamber.
G. — Culverts in side walls.
H. — Lateral culverts.

manipulating the gates and the valves and in propelling boats through the locks.

A ship passing south will enter the first lock at sea level; the gate behind it will then be closed and the first lock filled with water. This will raise the boat to a water level with the second lock, and so on. In passing north through the left series the order is reversed.

The danger of a boat's ramming the gates either by forward or by backward motion is guarded against in several ways. First, the boat will be drawn through the locks by electric locomotives running on the side walls. The stern of the boat will be controlled by two cables with power attachments, so

I. MONOLITHS IN MIDDLE WALL, UPPER GATUN, JULY, 1910
II. GATUN UPPER LOCKS, SHOWING GATE SILLS

that at any point the boat may be brought to a stand. This system of four cables likewise guards against any possibility of the lateral motion of the boat against the side and the middle walls. Second, the gates and the valves are operated by electric power and are as thoroughly under control as is the movement of the boat itself. Third, the higher level is separated from the level next below by two sets of gates. At each flight two barriers are thus provided. Fourth, above the upper gates are two movable dams or drawbridges which can be so manipulated as completely to cut off the water of the lake from the water of the locks.

Commenting on these various provisions against accidents, Commissioner Rousseau said in an address at Denver: "These devices have all been successfully tried, separately, on different locks in this country and abroad, but in no case has it ever been deemed necessary to install all of them in the same work." Referring to the first named safeguard, Mr. Rousseau continues: "Practically all recorded accidents to locks in recent years have occurred through some mistaking of signals between the pilot house and the engine-room while the vessel has been passing through locks under its own steam. To obviate this source of danger, it is proposed to provide on the walls of the locks electric locomotives, which under proper control will tow vessels through the locks, there being one locomotive on each side of the lock forward and astern, or four in all, vessels not being allowed to move their propellers meanwhile."

The gates are hollow steel structures seven feet thick and sixty-five feet long, and they vary in height and weight from forty-five to eighty-two feet and from three hundred to six hundred tons, respectively. Intermediate gates cut the locks into chambers four hundred and six hundred feet long. As over 90 per cent of the merchant ships of the world are under six hundred feet in length, this arrangement makes possible a great saving of water.

Adequate water supply is a subject of great importance and interest. The November visitor to the Zone who has seen the floods of the Chagres carrying before them trees, houses and bridges, submerging steam shovels, destroying miles of railroad, will never question the adequacy of the water supply. Somebody has said that in the Canal Zone there are two seasons of the year, the rainy and the wet. Still, it rains only occasionally during the months of January, February and March, and during the dry season of 1911–1912 there was very little rain from December first to May first. Decidedly there is a dry season here, and during this period of three months or more the average flow of the Chagres for the past twenty years has been something like six hundred cubic feet per second; while at one time

I. WEST CHAMBER, GATUN UPPER LOCKS, DECEMBER, 1910
II. FOREBAY AND LIFT SILL, GATUN LOCKS, MARCH, 1910

during that period it reached the very low figure of three hundred feet per second.

Besides the use of water for electrical power, the water supply will be drawn on in three ways — leakage, lockage and evaporation. It is estimated that the loss in these ways will be about three thousand feet per second. When the Chagres flow is at its minimum of three hundred feet per second there is a disparity between loss and supply of 2700 feet per second. The possible net loss in one day would be over 130,000,000 cubic feet, and in one month about 4,000,000,000 cubic feet. It must be remembered, however, in this connection that three hundred feet is the minimum flow of the river itself, and that these figures have not taken into account the discharge of its tributaries below Bohio. The slope of the land on the Isthmus is very sharp, and as a result the minimum flow is reached early in the dry season, and as that season lasts at times for over three months, it is obvious that in an enterprise of such magnitude as the Panama Canal, involving so large a part of the world's commerce, provision must be made against the possibility of any interruption from a shortage of water supply. This contingency is met by the large area, 164 square miles, of Gatun Lake. It provides ample storage capacity — losses from all sources are not likely to lower the lake more than three feet — while the canal will be usable after the lake has been lowered by five feet. In the very improbable event that future commerce should make demands on the lake beyond its estimated capacity, a dam which might be constructed at Alhajuela would furnish additional storage to be drawn upon in time of need.

On our way to lunch we shall pass the Administration Building of the Atlantic Division, the Commissary and Panama Railroad Depot, and the Y. M. C. A. Clubhouse. We will visit the Isthmian Canal Commission hotel for luncheon. The Jamaican waiter first serves us with soup of a choice variety, then with an A 1 steak, baked beans, mashed potatoes, salad, good bread, genuine butter, apple pie, of the variety mother makes, coffee and ice cream. You may top off the meal with a Gatun cocktail from that amber bottle if you like. Bitter? Well, yes, but you didn't give us time to explain. The cocktail is a solution of liquid quinine! You will find such a cocktail as this at every I. C. C. hotel.

After lunch let us take a special train across the line of the canal. From Gatun the old line, which long ago was taken up but on which we are to take our imaginary trip, winds its snaky way out through the jungles of the great Black Swamp. To right and left the impounded waters of the Chagres already spread out before us for miles. The cleared passage in the jungles to the right is the line of the canal. Little excavation is necessary here, for the

A TYPICAL LABOR TRAIN

land to Bohio is practically all below the grade line of the canal.

Take a look at nature now, while we are out of sight of the canal. Over there is a twenty-foot alligator, basking his huge bulk in the sun. Just beyond him are forty or fifty white cranes; wheeling above the water, now high, now low, are many varieties of sea birds, for we can still scent the salt sea. The train dashes into the jungles and we see "fronded palms," ferns, canebrakes, bamboo, wild bananas, lignum-vitæ with its gaudy dress, and myriads of botanical species garbed in purple, pink, red, white and gold. You may not see them, but these jungles teem with snakes, lizards, deer, jaguars, monkeys, wildcats, armadillos, tapirs, wild hogs, sloths and countless varieties of plant and animal life. Here and there a stream penetrates the otherwise impenetrable network of vegetable life to break the monotony of the fast moving panorama. Only at such intervals does one get an adequate notion of the grace and beauty of the tropics of Panama.

Bohio is called, and as our train slows down, the voice of the ever-present vender of bananas is heard, luring the hungry passenger to invest. Just as we pull out from the station, on the right side of the track, there is a funny little structure with a cylindrical brick foundation supporting a miniature house, reached by a long flight of stairs. This is the Bohio fluviograph station, and the river is the far famed Chagres. This is one of several stations along the river where records are made of the volume of water discharged by it. This one was installed by the French in 1890, and has been in use for more than twenty years. The fluviograph work comes under the Division of River Hydraulics, Meteorology and Surveys. The other three stations along the Chagres are at Gatun, Gamboa and Alhajuela. The importance of measuring the river's discharge has already been indicated. The other work of this division, as its name indicates, is the determination of the amount of rainfall and evaporation, and observations of seismological disturbances.

The table on page 71 summarizes the results of the observations of the Subdivision of Meteorology on the distribution of rainfall on the Canal Zone, showing hourly periods of maximum and minimum rainfall during an average year.

This table will help one to appreciate one of the greatest difficulties with which the Commission has had to contend, as well as the mathematical precision and the scientific method brought to bear on this great engineering proposition.

The station just called is Tabernilla. To the left is the Tabernilla dump. Here millions of cubic yards of dirt from Culebra Cut have been piled up. Had we passed this point in 1910 we should have

DISTRIBUTION OF RAINFALL

STATION	AVERAGE TOTAL RAINFALL IN INCHES	TOTAL RAINFALL FROM 7 A.M. TO 5 P.M.		MAXIMUM RAINFALL		MINIMUM RAINFALL	
		Amount in Inches	Per Cent of Total	Hour of Maximum	Accumulated Amount in Inches	Hour of Minimum	Accumulated Amount in Inches
Cristobal	137.71	67.32	49	1 to 2 P.M.	12.59	10 to 11 P.M.	1.79
Bohio	118.98	83.82	70	2 to 3 P.M.	14.81	9 to 10 P.M.	.82
Culebra	77.45	64.83	84	2 to 3 P.M.	16.04	9 to 10 P.M.	.28
Pedro Miguel	77.45	65.22	84	1 to 2 P.M.	17.57	9 to 10 P.M.	.22
La Boca	56.71	39.67	70	1 to 2 P.M.	8.96	3 to 4 A.M.	.30

seen dirt train after dirt train going out on this dump with its cargo from the Cut, unloading with its great plow. This plow will unload a dirt train of twenty-one cars, carrying more than six hundred tons of material, in less than fifteen minutes. The train just pulling out from the siding there is a typical labor train, which will carry out on the works some six hundred of the thirty-five thousand employees of the Commission.

Another very interesting piece of work which you could have seen here a little while ago is that of track shifting. Special machinery for this purpose has been put into service. As the track quickly gets out of reach of the edge of the dump, it becomes necessary to shift it. This is not done by taking it to pieces, for not a spike is lifted, not a bolt removed. The machine by which the process is performed is a track shifter. It lays hold of a section of track, picks it up bodily, and puts it in position again with very little ceremony. One of these machines is said to be capable of moving from one to two miles of track a day. It is manipulated by nine men and will do the work of six hundred laborers. There are ten of these big machines in the service of the Commission.

The man you see there with the queer little machine strapped on his back, and the two others just beyond him, are members of the small army whose

TRACK SHIFTING MACHINE

business it is to guard the large army of canal diggers against a flank attack of the enemy most dreaded in Panama — the mosquito. One man is spraying the sides of the ditch with larvacide; the other two are burning the grass along an open ditch to prevent the hatching of eggs deposited in these moist places by mosquitoes.

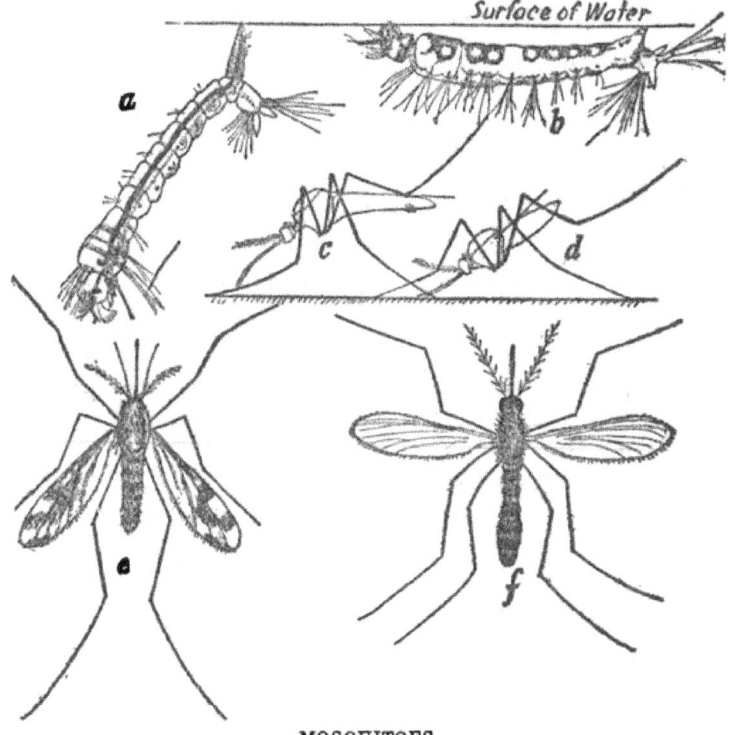

MOSQUITOES

Figures *a* and *b* show the larvae in water. At *c* is shown the position assumed by the harmless type (Culex) upon alighting, and at *d* the position of the dangerous one. At *e* is shown the Anopheles with spotted wings and five hair-like feelers in front; at *f* the Culex with plain wings and three feelers.

You will note by this time that we are following the valley of the Chagres. The conductor calls San Pablo just as we cross the bridge over this river. To the right there are signs of excavation. We are fast approaching the continental divide, and the shallow excavation observed is really the beginning of the great Cut. Just below San Pablo the railroad crosses the line of the canal and follows that line almost to the Pacific. If you will watch closely, you will see some old French dredges, long ago sunk to the bottom of the channel — silent reminders of the French failure. Such part of the old French machinery as is no longer of use to the Commission is sold to the highest bidder, as so much junk.

But remember that this first part of our trip is an imaginary one. For the route we have covered since leaving Gatun has been submerged for some time, and the people of the little towns we have passed fled long ago to the hills bordering the man-made Gatun Lake. Had we traversed the relocated line from Gatun to Gorgona, we should have seen many of them in their new homes. When warned of the rising floods, one old lady who had lived at Bohio for a half century, so the story goes, expressed, with a religious fervor to be envied by more enlightened Christians, her faith in the promise, "And the waters shall no more become a flood." She was, however, doomed to disappointment, for her little homestead, like thousands of others in the lake district, is now fathoms under water. The government has reimbursed her for the losses she sustained.

As we pass Gorgona, Matachin, Bas Obispo and Las Cascadas, we are rapidly coming to the crest of the continental divide. At Matachin the Chagres breaks off to the east, and we now leave its valley. In some remote geological age this river found its way through the divide somewhere near Culebra and poured its floods into the Pacific. The final upheaval which gave the Isthmus its present contour diverted the course of the Chagres to the north. Were it not to minimize the work of man, we might compare the present artificial diversion of this river with nature's diversion on the divide.

CHAPTER V

THE BIG CUT

It has already been said that the construction of the canal involved at once the greatest piece of constructive work and the greatest piece of destructive work ever undertaken by man. We have seen something of the constructive work, and we will now descend into Culebra Cut to see the other phase of this great work. We enter the Cut just below Matachin.

Note the solid stone walls on either side. Through this flint-like rock the workers have cut a channel three hundred feet wide at the bottom, and at places nearly two hundred feet deep. The depth of the Cut at various points is indicated in the diagram. In the Cut millions of pounds of the dynamite we saw unloading at Cristobal have been discharged. As we go up the Cut you may witness a blast of several tons which will displace thousands of yards of the granite-like mass, on which the steam shovels are set to work. You will notice at the top of the bank of rock and to the right several queer-looking machines. These are the compressed air drills manipulated by West Indians, and used in drill-

THE PAY CAR AT CULEBRA, JANUARY, 1908

CULEBRA SLIDE, WEST BANK LOOKING SOUTH, NOVEMBER, 1909

ing holes for the dynamite charges. The charges are detonated by means of electric connections, and it is done with such skill and care that accidents in the way of premature discharges, so common in the handling of explosives elsewhere, are now entirely relegated to the past.

As we pass up the Cut to the next point of attraction we may make some observations of interest.

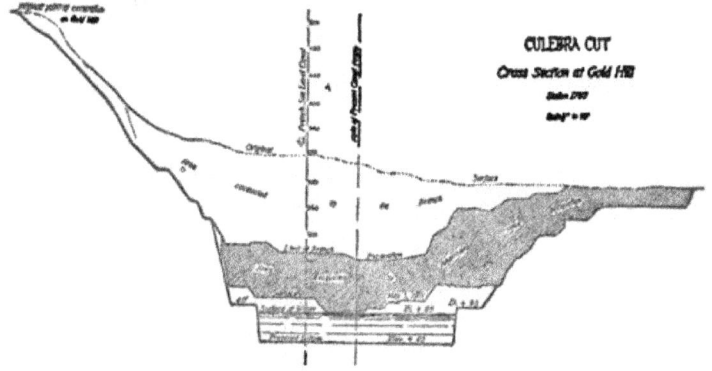

Culebra Cut begins at Bas Obispo and the excavation gradually increases in depth for a distance of about five miles to Gold Hill, where it reaches the maximum elevation of 534 feet on the east bank, 312 feet on the center line, and 410 feet on the west bank. (See diagram above.) At Gold Hill, Culebra, the Pacific slope begins, and the Cut continues down the southern incline to Pedro Miguel, a distance of three miles. While the Cut proper, as the engineers define it, is said to be nine miles in length, the excavation is continuous from San Pablo to Pedro Miguel, a distance of sixteen miles. The amount of excavation throughout this distance in the Cut is estimated at something near 100,000,000 cubic yards, equivalent to a mound of earth three hundred feet high, three hundred yards wide, and two miles long. The total excavation for the canal is estimated at nearly 200,000,000 cubic yards. You may now extend our little mound two miles farther. To make these figures more concrete, imagine a team of horses and the ordinary one-yard gravel wagon at work moving this dirt an average distance of twenty miles, and you have the size of the job.

You will notice that the banks of the canal on either side are rising higher above us. We are approaching Culebra. The suspension bridge over the canal at Empire hangs high above our track, and still the side walls of the canal are rising. The hills rising beyond Culebra are the famous Gold Hill and Contractor's Hill. Through these the steam shovels are gradually but surely cutting their way. Many obstacles present themselves, but all are insignificant in comparison to the one in evidence yonder — the famous Culebra slide, which, like the mighty American glaciers of days gone by, is working its way, inch by inch, toward the prism of the canal. It is now estimated that this and other slides involve the removal of an extra seventeen million cubic yards

STEAM SHOVEL LOADING ROCK, CULEBRA CUT

I. BOTTOM OF CANAL RAISED EIGHTEEN FEET THROUGH PRESSURE OF THE BROKEN EAST BANK, JUNE, 1910
II. CULEBRA CUT FROM CONTRACTOR'S HILL, APRIL, 1910

of dirt. The bulk just in front of us is only one of many subsidiary slides — the mere breaking off from the main bulk of huge chunks which tumble into the Cut like avalanches, burying steam shovels, cars, locomotives, tracks, everything in their way. There are two kinds of slides; those which slowly and imperceptibly move toward the Cut, such as the largest Culebra slide, covering an area of nearly thirty acres, and the Cucaracha slide, covering an area of about fifty acres; and those that break off and topple over precipitately into the Cut. The latter are insignificant in point of size as compared with the former. The total area involved by the slides in Culebra Cut is one hundred and sixty acres, equal in area to a good-sized farm in the States. The Cucaracha slide began moving in 1884, or twenty-eight years ago.

The Culebra and Cucaracha slides are the most notable among the obstacles to the speedy completion of the work in the Central or Culebra Division. These caused Colonel Goethals to say in an interview in New York that the only significant elements in the uncertainty as to the date of the completion of the canal are the two big slides, and the obstacles growing out of them. The mound of earth there in the middle of the prism and to the left of our tracks is one of these obstacles. The mound is the result of the buckling of the bottom of the prism, supposed to have been caused by the pressure of the broken east bank.

If you could brave the tropical sun and make the climb to the top of Gold Hill, you would get a splendid view of the Cut, and such an appreciation of the magnitude of the work as you could not otherwise get. Here the canal makers have had to cut through solid rock for a distance of nearly five hundred feet.

By climbing these steps we shall come up into the town of Culebra, and incidentally get, through the muscular sense, a concrete notion of the depth of the Cut. As we come out on level ground we may get a second concrete notion of the magnitude of the work, for it is near the middle of the month, and the pay car has arrived to present "the laborer with his hire." From one end of the Zone to the other this train goes on its errand each month, distributing the earnings of the makers of the canal.

Before we leave this spot, notice the big steam shovels at work below us. They seem almost human when at work. Under favorable conditions the big fellow there will load a Lidgerwood car in about two minutes, and a whole train of cars in less than fifty minutes. Watch him as he dips down for his mouthful of dirt, then watch him hoist the seven or eight tons of clay and rock, swing it over to the car, and deposit it again with less show of effort than would be displayed by a boy with his toy shovel.

A SEAGOING SUCTION DREDGE

I. PEDRO MIGUEL LOCKS LOOKING SOUTH, AUGUST, 1910
II. PEDRO MIGUEL LOCKS LOOKING NORTH, NOVEMBER, 1910

As we pass out onto the main street of Culebra we come into full view of the Administration Building. Here are the offices of the Chairman and Chief Engineer of the Commission.

Our special train will now take us down the main line past old Paraiso, where the Panama Railroad recrosses the canal. Looking south from the bridge we get a view of the huge berm cranes spanning the locks at Pedro Miguel. A nearer approach will reveal the fact that the locks at this end of the canal practically duplicate those at Gatun, except that the first flight is separated from the second and third flights, a distance of two miles, by Miraflores Lake.

The Pedro Miguel locks really mark the foot of Culebra Cut, for from Pedro Miguel to Miraflores comparatively little excavation has been necessary. The canal descends to sea level at Miraflores, and most of the excavation from here to deep water in the Pacific is below sea level. We can take a dredge from here to La Boca, at the Pacific entrance. There is the "Culebra," one of the largest suction dredges in the service. As it is just now ready to leave with its great load of mud, we will go with it far out into the Pacific. As we pass out of the Pacific entrance, the Balboa docks will be the first point of interest. This is the southern freight terminal of the Panama Railroad, which has for more than half a century received the commerce of the Pacific, to redeposit it in the Atlantic steamers at Colon, bound for eastern America and Europe. Our boat will carry us near Flamenco Island, which is soon to become the Gibraltar of the New World. The dredge will deposit its burden in the deep waters of the "South Sea." To our left is Culebra Island, where the Pacific quarantine station is located.

From the vicinity of Flamenco Island we may see a score of small islands lying at the Pacific entrance of the canal. As we again approach Balboa on our return trip, we note a flat looking boat at the docks in front of us. This is a sand barge from Chame, and the machinery which is relieving it of its burden is a Cleveland crane unloader.

The drive from Balboa into Ancon will be an interesting one. We come around the north side of Sosa Hill and into full view of Mount Ancon. Around the foot of this hill is one of the prettiest drives one could find anywhere. The macadamized road, palms of a hundred varieties, mango trees, coconut trees, Chinese gardens, historic Ancon Hill, the blue Pacific stretching away to the horizon, the cool evening breezes, the quaint Spanish suburbs of the typical Spanish city of Panama — all combine to make this three-mile drive a most pleasant and interesting one; and when you arrive at Ancon, you will be prepared to do justice to the sumptuous dinner provided for you at the Tivoli Hotel.

ON THE WAY FROM BALBOA TO ANCON

HOTEL TIVOLI

Standing on an eminence above the city of Panama the Tivoli Hotel commands a magnificent view of the mountains to the northeast. We are, indeed, in a land of countless manifestations of nature's power and diversity — a land where history lends its interest to every hilltop, and romance its charm to every valley. Away to the east, on, on, on, and out of sight, stretches the Pacific like a sea of glass, guarded on the left by the blue ranges that the buccaneers of centuries ago scaled in their search of wealth; that Balboa climbed in quest of the South Sea and eternal fame; that Pizarro crossed in his march toward the land of the Incas. In the midst of your reverie you are awakened by the sudden lighting up of the whole sky. The green of the nearby hills and the blue of the distant mountains are slowly transformed, now into purple, now into violet, and then finally into an almost invisible gray. When at last you turn your eyes in the direction of the source of all this splendor, you behold a sunset so splendid as to make one feel that nature herself, despairing of words, is giving utterance to her emotions in this wild, inarticulate harmony of colors. Resting upon the hills that border the Pacific to the west is a great billowy cloud fringed at its lower edge with a brilliant crimson, and undulating into myriad flames of scarlet, orange and gold. Above the cloud for some distance is clear sky — not blue, but liquid emerald; then again there are light fleecy clouds of delicate pink, imperceptibly fading as they recede toward the darkness. At last the landscape sinks back into night's embrace. After a day's strenuous observation you have probably dismissed from your mind the idea that the canal diggers are outside the pale of civilization.

Our imaginary trip has taken us across the Isthmus at the most interesting stage of the work. But remember that it is all a dream, for things happen so fast in the Canal Zone that what is news to-day is history to-morrow. Some of the ground we have covered is now under the waters of Gatun Lake.

THE ISTHMIAN CANAL COMMISSION

CHAPTER VI

ORGANIZATION

To the tourist crossing the Isthmus one thing is everywhere in evidence — effective organization. As David Starr Jordan says, "The world stands aside to let the man pass who knows where he is going." The men here know both where they are going and when they will arrive. Never before have so many experts been called together on one piece of work. The Panama Canal will stand as the product of American genius and as a monument to thousands of intelligent Americans who knew their business.

Mention has been made of the treaty under which the United States acquired control of the territory known as the Canal Zone. The necessity for such an arrangement was obvious. All obstacles which might be put in the way of the construction work and the general administration of affairs were wisely anticipated by the provision giving the United States government absolute jurisdiction over a strip of territory extending five miles on either side of the line of the canal, and the right to the use of any territory adjacent thereto which might be made to contribute to the construction and operation of the canal. In other words, it was intended that there should be nothing to do but to "go ahead" when the Commission began the work of actual digging.

While some departments have been absorbed by others, and while new departments have been created, the organization has not been changed in any essential feature since the beginning of the undertaking, though the same cannot be said of the personnel. In 1904 the Commission was organized under the Department of War of the United States and has continued its operations under that department. The diagram opposite will indicate the general plan of organization.

It will be noted that the Panama Railroad is not included in this diagram. The omission is due to the fact that the railroad, though owned by the government, is operated as a private corporation; such an arrangement permits the company to sue and to be sued, and to continue the passenger and freight traffic which it has built up. Any arrangement which resulted in discontinuing this traffic would have been a serious menace to the commerce which has taken this route for a half century. Besides this advantage to those interested in transisthmian commerce, the company has continued to earn a large dividend for the government.

For some time prior to 1904 the road was handling, annually, traffic averaging nearly 20,000,000 ton-

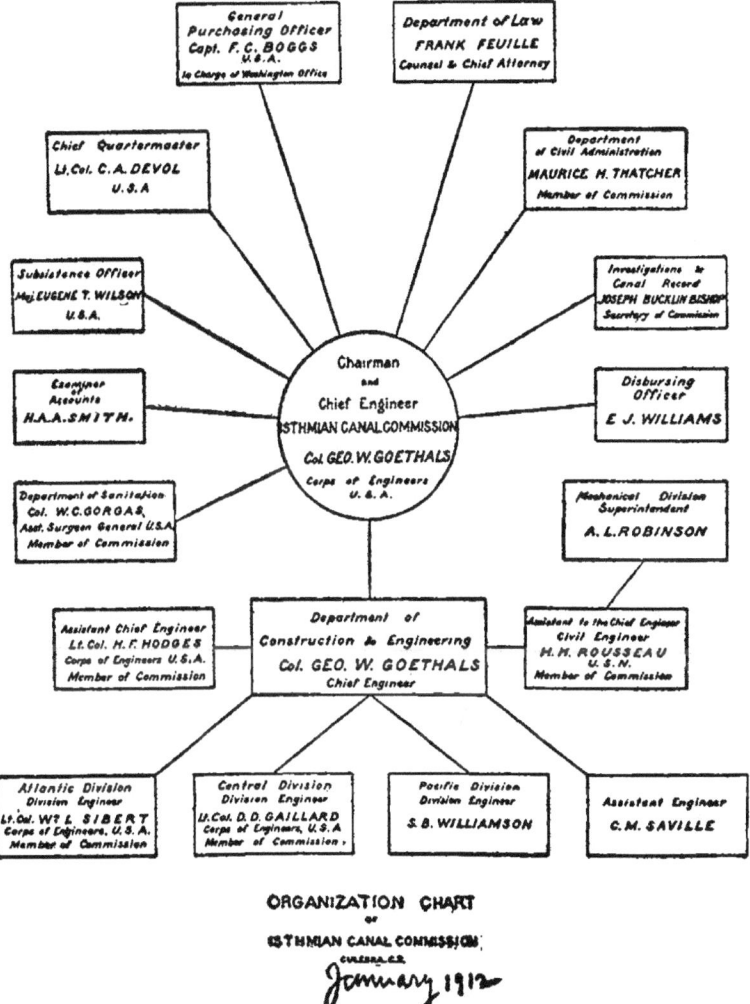

miles. The additions incident to the Commission's work increased the amount to 280,000,000 ton-miles. Such an enormous increase necessitated much reconstruction. As the road followed the line of the canal, practically all of the roadbed from Gatun to Bas Obispo would be submerged on the completion of the dam, and the relocation of many other miles of the road was necessary. To meet the increased demands of transportation about thirty-seven miles of the road were double-tracked; to get out of Gatun Lake and to avoid crossing the canal another thirty-seven miles of road have been relocated. The double tracking was accomplished early in the history of the work under American control. The relocated line was completed in 1912 at a cost of about $9,000,000. The old line from Gatun to Gorgona, a distance of twenty miles, was taken up in the early part of the year, and its bed will soon be forty feet below the surface of the now fast rising Gatun Lake.

CHAPTER VII

QUARTERMASTER'S DEPARTMENT

THE organization in this department includes the Chief Quartermaster, Assistant Chief Quartermaster, Depot Quartermaster, Constructing Quartermaster, eleven District Quartermasters, six Storekeepers, two hundred and twenty-one "gold" employees and over three thousand "silver" employees. The Department was organized in July, 1908, by Colonel C. A. Devol, U.S.A. Its business may be summarized as follows: (1) to recruit all unskilled labor for the work; (2) to assign, furnish and take charge of all commission quarters; (3) to execute the orders of the Sanitary Department in matters relating to grass cutting and the removal of *débris;* (4) to construct and to repair all Isthmian Canal Commission buildings; (5) to make requisition for and to distribute all supplies for the Commission; (6) to "scrap" the old French material; and (7) to audit all property returns pertaining to the business of the Commission.

Colonel Devol says in his annual report: "The administration of the various districts by District and Assistant District Quartermasters is an evolution from the administration of an army post. In each case the Quartermaster attends to all material wants of the community except food supplies. Even these latter are delivered from the Commissaries to the consumers by this department. Each district has a small working force of artisans, utility men, janitors, etc., to attend to the wants of the district, and maintains a corral with a sufficient number of animals and vehicles for local needs."

The 39,000 employees of the Commission and of the Panama Railroad are classified under the two general heads, "gold" and "silver;" and quarters are classified under the same heads. Assignments are made by the District Quartermasters in accordance with an established code of rules, based on the date of application, rate of salary and date of entry into the service. The rules governing assignments have stood the test of time, and it is seldom that complaints go above the Quartermaster in charge of the district.

The quarters, both for bachelors and for married men, are furnished by the Government, and fuel, light and water are supplied without charge. These allowances for the married men and for the bachelors differ somewhat; the table on page 103 gives the monthly allowances *per capita*.

From this table it will be observed that married employees receive benefits beyond their stipulated salaries amounting to something like $40 per month, while the benefits received by the bachelor employees amount to about $14 per month. The quarters are all provided with modern plumbing

MONTHLY ALLOWANCES	MARRIED MEN	BACHELORS
Fuel	$3.30	$0.00
Light	5.13	.57
Water	1.25	.26
Garbage, and care of	1.51	.15
Janitor service	0.00	1.25
Free transportation	1.00	1.00
Y.M.C.A. and Band	.75	.75
Medical attendance	7.50	5.00
Saving of Rent	20.00	5.00
	$40.44	$13.98

and with necessary furniture. Assignment to married quarters is graded as to the class of houses as follows: Employees drawing less than $200 a month are assigned to four-family houses, known as Type 14; those drawing from $200 to $300 a month, to cottages known as Types 15 and 17, and to two-family houses known as Type 19; those drawing between $300 and $400 to two-story one-family houses known as Type 10; from $400 up, assignments are made to official class houses, of which there are several types.

"Silver" bachelor employees are housed in barracks, each accommodating seventy-two men. The barrack system is modeled directly after the United States Army transport plan. The barracks are equipped with bunks of the triple standee type, fitted with laced bunk bottoms. The barracks are in charge of janitors, who clean them each day. The trunks and the effects of the laborers are kept on broad shelves, no bundles or baggage of any kind being permitted on the floors. The floors are thoroughly scrubbed twice each week, and once every twenty days all bunk bottoms are taken out and boiled.

As stated elsewhere, Young Men's Christian Association clubhouses are maintained in the large towns along the line of the work. There are seven of these buildings, located at Cristobal, Gatun, Gorgona, Empire, Culebra, Corozal and Porto Bello. In them employees are given additional facilities for social, church and lodge functions.

The ornamentation of the grounds about "gold" quarters and about the public buildings is carried on systematically by gardeners under the District Quartermasters. A propagating garden is maintained at Empire, from which plants are distributed. The Quartermaster's Department provides, free of charge, to all "gold" employees, such plants as they desire for ornamenting the premises about their quarters.

I. SLEEPING QUARTERS FOR NEGROES (105)
II. LABOR QUARTERS

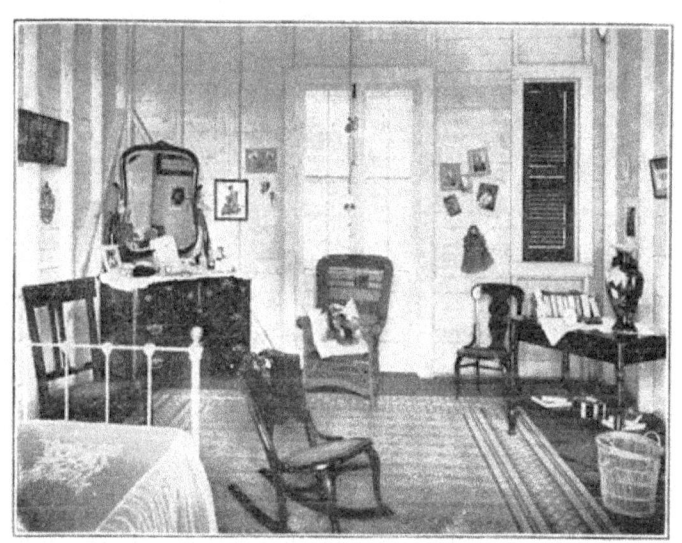

I. A BEDROOM IN FAMILY QUARTERS
II. Y. M. C. A. CLUBHOUSE

As plants grow luxuriantly in the tropics, most of the yards about the quarters present an appearance which would be the envy of any professional horticulturist in the United States. There are few houses that are not surrounded with a luxuriant growth of flowers, shrubs and vines. Indeed, the employees, bachelor and married, are provided with quarters which often exceed in furnishings, both inside and out, those to which they were accustomed before coming to the Isthmus.

The Building and Construction Division is organized with a small force in each district. In addition to these forces there are what are known as traveling gangs — four carpenter gangs and three painting gangs. It is the business of these men, together with those employed in each district, to construct all new buildings not built under contract and to maintain the three thousand buildings in the Canal Zone. The buildings already constructed have cost about eleven million dollars, their upkeep averaging a yearly outlay of about two hundred and fifty thousand dollars, which is about two and one half per cent of their valuation.

The materials and supplies for the work on the canal requisitioned through the Quartermaster's Department amount to about eleven million dollars annually, while the stock on hand at all the storehouses is estimated to be worth nearly five million dollars. When it is remembered that this material has to be carried by ship for a distance of two thousand miles and that the stock includes railway supplies, steam shovel supplies, and all the diversified handling plants, this amount does not seem excessive. The price book published by the department itemizes more than twenty thousand articles, and it is required of the department that it meet every emergency. Quite a complicated business, this!

All purchases and contracts for supplies must be advertised in sufficient time to admit of fair competition. It is, therefore, necessary to allow for at least a three months' interval between the making of a requisition and the receipt of the supplies, except in emergency cases, when the law permits purchase in open market.

The storehouse system begins at Mount Hope, the storehouse there being known as the Quartermaster's Depot. The accountability for all property is initiated at Mount Hope, where the United States bills are certified and the supplies become government property. From Mount Hope to the line storehouses the material is handled by a system of invoices and receipts. Each article of government property is carried on a physical accountability system. Returns are rendered to the Chief Quartermaster every six months; the audit of these returns by cross check from the return of one storehouse to that of another storehouse constitutes a debit and credit material account for all officers carrying property responsibility.

The "scrapping" of French material by the Quartermaster's Department consists of the disposal of some one hundred thousand tons of old French junk. About two thousand tons are sent each month to the United States on the cement ships *Ancon* and *Cristobal*, thus giving these boats a ballasting cargo when north bound.

The Department has in its service about six hundred mules and horses, distributed among the corrals of the different districts. This provides for all team service on the Canal Zone, teams and drivers being furnished to the Construction and other Divisions for $3.50 a day.

It may be stated, in conclusion, that the Quartermaster's Department on the Isthmus is to the Canal Zone work what the Quartermaster's Department in the United States is to the Army, both in the United States and in its island possessions, except that the Quartermaster's Department on the Isthmus has a cost-keeping system, and the provision and maintenance of a construction plant, and the supply of material, which does not pertain to army administration. In a word, the system is a combination of army and railroad practice, with the best and most applicable features in each retained.

Under this system, material matters pertaining to an annual appropriation of more than forty million dollars are successfully taken care of, and more than thirty-nine thousand employees of more than thirty distinct nationalities and races are housed and made contented and comfortable. The work of the Quartermaster's Department is as efficient as it is important and complicated.

CHAPTER VIII

SANITATION

ONE of the chief causes of the failure of the French in their canal project was inadequate sanitation. The chief diseases with which the French had to contend were malaria, yellow fever and smallpox. In those days the cities of Colon and Panama were breeding places for these and for other diseases. The streets and the sidewalks were not paved, and during the "rainy season," which lasts for nine months in the year, they were practically impassable. Add to these conditions the absence of electric lights and of plumbing, and you may have some appreciation of conditions in Panama and Colon as they were before American occupation. The first work of the United States was to clean up these towns. Wisely enough our government had anticipated this necessity in the treaty of 1904, by which we were given sanitary jurisdiction over the two terminal cities.

The Department of Sanitation immediately set to work, with results which seem miraculous. Today, driving leisurely down Central Avenue, Panama, one almost refuses to believe that a decade ago in place of the paved streets there was a mass of mud and filth for nine months of the year, impassable except on foot, and then only at the risk of besmirching one's self with filth thrown from the upper stories of the buildings adjacent to the street. One sees now what would be seen in any up-to-date city in the United States — electric lights, clean streets paved with vitrified brick, a water and a sewerage system and every modern urban convenience. These improvements, with the exception of the electric lights, were all made and paid for by the United States at a cost of about $3,000,000, under the agreement that Panama and Colon should refund the original cost by means of water rentals. The water and sewerage systems are maintained and operated by the Division of Public Works, a subordinate branch of the Canal Zone Department of Civil Administration. The cities of Panama and Colon have been given fifty years in which to liquidate this obligation. Without fear one may to-day quench his thirst at any hydrant in either city, for the crystal lakes which furnish the water supply are far away in the mountains, out of the reach of contagion.

The Canal Zone Sanitary Department has absolute authority in directing sanitary activities in the two cities. A Health Officer is appointed for each of the cities, whose business it is to enforce

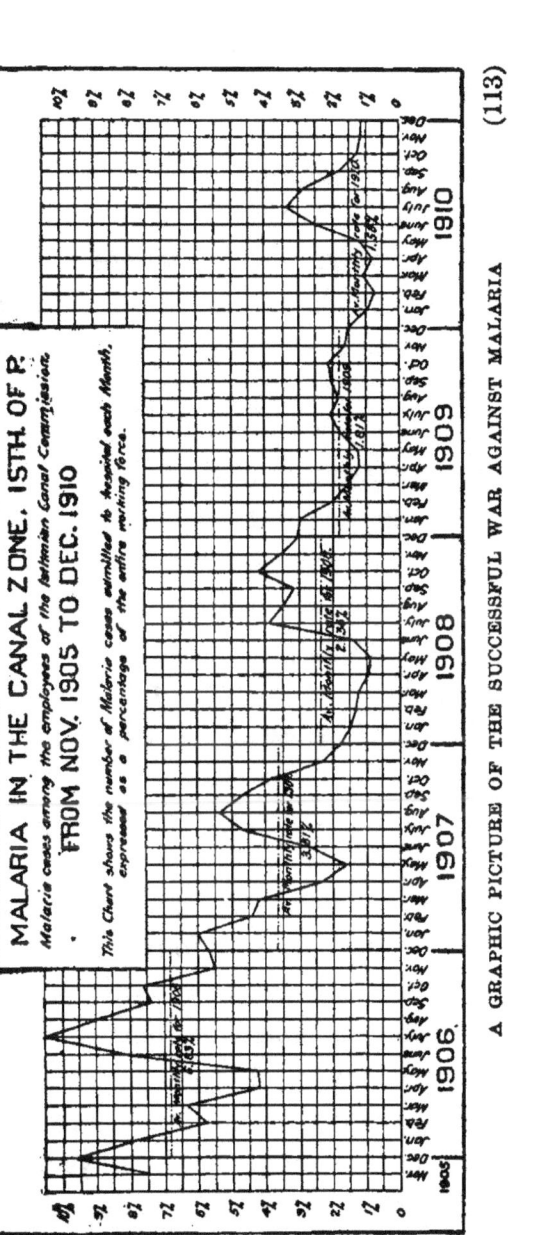

A GRAPHIC PICTURE OF THE SUCCESSFUL WAR AGAINST MALARIA

cleanliness and all sanitary measures which the head of the department may see fit to promulgate.

The work of cleaning up the cities was not all that had to be done. Doctor Gorgas, Chief Sanitary Officer, had discovered in Cuba, where he had learned to "sanitate," that cleanliness seemed to have little relationship to malaria and yellow fever, two of the deadliest enemies to the workmen in Panama. Vaccination would rid the country of smallpox; the destruction of rats minimized the possibilities of an attack of the plague; but clean up Havana as he would, malaria and yellow fever persisted. In fact, as Doctor Gorgas puts it, the cleaner he got the city, the greater the spread of the infection, "until it was discovered by Doctors Finley and Ross that there were two kinds of mosquitoes responsible for the transmission of these maladies" — the Stegomyia and the Anopheles, carriers, respectively, of yellow fever and of malaria.

Now it happens that the Stegomyia is quite domestic in its habits, and is never found far distant from man's habitation. It may be said that the little fellow is perfectly harmless so long as there are no cases of yellow fever in the community. It is merely a carrier, and its bite is as harmless as that of any mosquito until ten or twelve days have elapsed after it has bitten an infected person. By this time it has contracted the disease itself and is capable of communicating it. Nor is there danger of contagion from yellow fever by contact. One may safely sleep in a room with a yellow fever patient, provided there are no Stegomyias present. The three necessary conditions for infection are: (1) the presence of an infected human being; (2) the presence of the female Stegomyia; (3) the biting of the infected person, and the biting of a second person by the same mosquito, ten or twelve days later. In the absence of any one of these conditions, the transmission of yellow fever is impossible.

The work of sanitation on the Isthmus began in the early part of the year 1904. The French had been powerless to cope with the situation, especially as in their day the mode of transmission of yellow fever and malaria had not been discovered. The mosquito invaded the homes of the high and the low alike. The French had unwittingly furnished the Stegomyia with ideal breeding places, constructing for it elaborate homes in the way of concrete pools which were intended as reservoirs for decorative plants, but which were appropriated by the enterprising little insect as a place most fitting for propagation. From these aristocratic quarters it went forth at night on its deadly errand, and ere the light of the next day drove it again to its hiding place its homicidal work was accomplished.

The swamps, cesspools, and sluggish streams near

the quartering places were given no attention by the French, and these furnished natural breeding places for the Anopheles, the carrier of malaria.

Obviously, the first work of the Department of Sanitation was to take measures against these formidable foes. So rain barrels, cisterns and all water containers were made mosquito proof with wire screening, cesspools were either drained or oiled, and the jungles near the thickly populated places were cleared to expose the hidden breeding places of the mosquito. All patients suspected of yellow fever infection were removed to the fever wards, which were carefully screened. As a further precaution against infection within the wards themselves, each patient was in turn screened in, so that the yellow fever ward appeared more like a menagerie of caged human beings than a place of human habitation. The homes from which such patients were taken were always fumigated. A little later the plan of screening all Commission houses was carried into effect. The result of all these curative and preventive measures was the extermination of yellow fever, the last case of infection on the Isthmus occurring in September, 1905.

Fortunately the Stegomyia's travels are very limited. In a lifetime it seldom journeys more than one hundred yards. It breeds in fresh, clear water, rather than in cesspools, and is never found in moving streams. But wherever it finds the least bit of water to its liking, there it takes up its abode. Mr. Le Prince, Chief Sanitary Inspector, says: "We have even found the larvæ in water tanks on locomotives, and in depressions in castings or parts of cars used for the transportation of rock and dirt. The adults are apt to collect where water or dampness is present, and have been found in bathrooms." It is easy to see how eternal vigilance is the price for the extermination of so persistent an enemy. In the instructions to sanitary inspectors occurs this paragraph, which describes the Stegomyia: —

"The lyre-shaped mark on the back is clearly shown, and it must be borne in mind that no other mosquito has these marks nor any resembling them, even though you may find pale marks on a dark ground. A few Stegomyia have the ground color pale, even light brownish, but the lyre is there. White banded legs and transverse bars on the abdomen have no significance if the lyre-shaped mark is absent."

After yellow fever, malaria has been the most dreaded of tropical maladies, not so much for its fatality as for its persistent prevalence, and because of its serious obstruction to work. Much the same preventive measures were adopted in the case of the malaria-carrying Anopheles as in that of the Stegomyia. Drainage, oiling, cutting of grass and clearing of jungle growth have been the chief preventives. The effectiveness with which the Sanitary Department did its work along this line is shown by the table on page 121.

But clean up as much as they would, it was found that people were still taken ill. Moreover, in the canal work many people were necessarily injured. So there was need for the splendid hospital service which is maintained under the direction of the Department of Sanitation. There are two hospitals, one at Colon, the other at Ancon — the latter being one of the largest and best equipped in the world. Here every disease to which man is heir is skillfully treated. There are the operating wards, the insane wards, the fever wards, the maternity ward, the tuberculosis wards, isolation wards and so on. The hospital has fifty buildings in all, and a capacity of fifteen hundred patients. The average number treated annually since American occupation has been 23,600, or a total of more than 188,000 patients.

The organization of the Sanitary Department is much like that of an army. The Zone was divided into districts, each with its district inspector and district physician. Through these lieutenants the war against disease has continued for eight years, with such results as the world knows. Every village and city of the Canal Zone has its district physician

BURNING GRASS FROM SIDES OF A DITCH

APPLYING LARVACIDE WITH KNAPSACK SPRAY

I. ENTRANCE TO ANCON HOSPITAL GROUNDS (120)
II. I. C. C. SANITARIUM AT TABOGA

POPULATION AND DEATH RATE

City of Panama

1884–1910

YEARS	POPULATION	YELLOW FEVER	BERI-BERI	TUBERCULOSIS	MALARIA	TYPHOID FEVER	SMALL-POX	OTHER DISEASES	TOTAL	ANNUAL DEATH RATE PER M.
1884–1886	21,000	523	0	347	1675	75	22	3757	6399	101
1887–1889	21,000	374	79	378	1178	52	235	4522	6818	108
1890–1892	22,000	18	22	459	517	19	11	1764	2810	42
1893–1895	22,000	1	3	410	429	7	5	1699	2554	38
1896–1898	23,000	45	57	454	530	12	2	2210	3310	50
1899–1901	24,000	181	128	474	508	16	126	2389	3822	53
1902–1904	25,000	261	202	505	902	2	194	2837	4903	65
1905–1907	28,000	23	202	399	1401	17	0	1444	3486	41
1908–1910	35,000	1[1]	95	471	429	13	0	2471	3480	33

[1] Brought in from Cartagena.

and dispensary. People with minor maladies are treated by these local physicians and are sent to the hospitals only when, in the opinion of such physicians, the condition of the patient requires hospital treatment. All this service is furnished free to employees, and at a nominal cost to their families.

A necessary adjunct to the hospital is the sanitarium at Taboga, where convalescents go for rest and recuperation. Taboga is one of the most healthful places in the world.

To the west of Taboga may be seen the leper colony of Palo Seco. There are usually about half a hundred patients in this dread place. On one occasion the superintendent of this hospital visited the office of the Superintendent of Schools in behalf of a little twelve-year-old boy on whom the gates of Palo Seco had closed. A pathetic errand, indeed, for he came with a message that the little fellow wanted some books to read. In his caged up condition it was thought the boy might like some elementary books on geography and history. These with others were sent to him. A few weeks later the hospital superintendent again returned on behalf of the little fellow, who wanted to know if he could have more books when he had read those sent him. Of course he could have all the books he wanted; but when the hospital superintendent again returned, he brought the message that the little soul had, after a brave but hopeless fight, succumbed to the terrible scourge. Though the shadows of darkness gathered fast about this little man, he had yet felt the impulse for light and struggled upward.

CHAPTER IX

SUBSISTENCE DEPARTMENT

If the Sanitary and the Quartermaster's Departments are essential and basal, no less may be said of the Subsistence Department. For if good men and true — men expert in their respective lines — were to be secured and held permanently, they must be guaranteed not only sanitary conditions and adequate living facilities, but also first-class food supplies.

As early as 1905 it became apparent that the food products of Panama would be inadequate to meet the demands of Americans entering the canal service. The food supply was scant and prices were exorbitant, but it was not until the middle of the year 1906 that any well directed effort was made to relieve the situation. During this year, however, hotels and messes were established in all the larger communities along the line of the canal. At the close of the year there were fourteen such conveniences. At first the Commission was undecided whether to handle subsistence direct, or by contract; but by the end of the year the plan of direct handling had demonstrated its wisdom, and the government decided to establish a Department of Subsistence in connection with the Commissary Department of the Panama Railroad.

At present this department handles everything that pertains to the feeding and clothing of the employees of the Commission. In his report for the year 1910, Major Wilson classifies the work of subsistence under four general heads: (1) Purchase and shipping; (2) Receiving and distribution; (3) Method of selling to employees; (4) Manufacturing.

All material handled by the department is purchased on contract through purchasing officers stationed in the cities of New York, New Orleans and San Francisco, and through agents abroad. The needs of the department are figured out some two months ahead of the actual demand, so that the purchasing agents may have ample time to advertise for bids. By this plan there is opportunity for competition, and competition which is both honest and sharp, as the prices of staples will indicate. All shipments from San Francisco are made by water. Very large requisitions have made competition so sharp that California food products may be obtained by the consumer on the Isthmus at as low a figure as the same may be purchased under the very shadow of the Californian's "own vine and fig tree!" The fact is that the employee on the Zone has access to a grocery as well stocked and up-to-date as those open to any citizen of Chicago. He gets strawberries, raspberries, blackberries, apples, grapes, pears, peaches, new potatoes — everything in season; and it is all good, for it has back of it a bonded guarantee which the United States will enforce even to the quality of a quart of strawberries.

The meats furnished are not inferior in quality nor higher in price than are those sold on the Chicago market. Of course, the meats are all from cold storage, but they are in every way as palatable as those that may be bought direct from the best retailers in the city meat markets of the United States. Meats sent from Chicago come the entire three thousand miles in a temperature considerably below freezing, and are put into the consumer's hands in even better condition for consumption than when they enter storage in that city.

A typical Isthmian dinner would consist of an A-grade porterhouse steak, potatoes, fresh country butter, homemade or fresh baker's bread, lettuce salad, peaches, cake and ice cream; or any modification of this bill of fare which the most cultivated taste of a northerner could devise or his purse afford.

Below is given a table which will indicate the culinary possibilities placed at the disposal of those employed on the Isthmus, together with the aggregate quantities of food used during the year 1910.

TABLE SUPPLIES

	Pounds
Peas and Beans (bulk)	1,128,792
Cocoa	109,504
Sugar	3,612,768
Tea	80,965
Baking Powders	39,922
Salmon	162,960
Preserved Fruit	766,623
Jams, Jellies, etc.	195,199
Meats (canned)	675,852
Milk (evaporated and condensed)	2,221,032
Tomatoes (in tins)	677,278
Pork and Beans (in tins)	77,278
Peas and Beans (in tins)	471,452
Other Vegetables (in tins)	524,069
Pickles and Sauces	169,460
Codfish	597,516
Pickled Fish	27,250
Flour	5,363,574
Rice	1,629,558
Cereals not otherwise specified	412,429
Biscuits	364,982
Confectionery	188,319
Lard	420,110
Fresh Meats	5,229,306
Cured and Pickled Meats	1,046,029
Cheese	114,192
Eggs	dozen 502,950
Butter	471,551
Poultry	429,575

Fresh Milk	gallons 41,901
Fresh Cream	gallons 22,900
Potatoes (Irish)	4,586,967
Potatoes (sweet)	638,584
Onions	717,557
Turnips	122,632
Beets	22,059
Carrots	91,830
Cabbage	656,905
Yams	424,789
Other Vegetables	622,484
Apples, Peaches, Pears	602,196
Plums, Grapes	71,772
Lemons, Grapefruit, Limes	dozen 267,758
Cantaloupes and Watermelons	pieces 70,569
Other Fruits	26,276

This bill of goods, taken from the annual report of the head of the department, would indicate that there are many mouths to feed, and that the United States has not only a good sized store, but that it is well stocked. The annual sales aggregate in value five and one third million dollars.

There is the same satisfactory service in the matter of clothing. All the wearing apparel required may be purchased at the local commissaries. Ready-made clothing, hats, ties, shirts, collars, shoes, boots, dress patterns, laces, silks, serges, worsteds — everything that a man or a woman can buy in the best department stores of the larger cities of the United States — can be purchased, the only difference being

MEAL TIME AT AN I. C. C. KITCHEN

in the lower prices paid on the Zone for articles of like quality.

All goods are held in the wholesale department at Cristobal till demand is made by the division storehouses along the line of the canal. Something of the magnitude of the business done by this department may be appreciated when it is stated that a train of twenty-one cars leaves Cristobal daily to distribute goods to the various branch commissaries on the Zone. These goods are received by the local commissaries, which in turn distribute them to the consumers by means of delivery wagons.

All purchases are made with commissary coupon books. These books are issued to employees by the various departments, the amounts they represent being deducted from the monthly salary of the recipient. Money will not be received in payment for goods purchased. Such a plan prevents the purchase of goods by non-employees, an arrangement which is necessary in order to carry out the spirit of the clause in the treaty with Panama about protecting her merchants against competition with government prices.

CHAPTER X

DEPARTMENT OF CIVIL ADMINISTRATION

NOTHING illustrates better the policy of the United States government in this great undertaking than does the organization of the Civil Department. At its opening meeting the Isthmian Canal Commission declared the building of the canal to be a purely industrial proposition, and to this day there has been no deviation from the policy implied in that statement. That this industrial proposition might be met and solved satisfactorily, it must have a social basis. Desirable workmen would not be attracted to a society where there were none of those amenities which they enjoyed in their native land.

It was no philanthropic motive which actuated the men in charge to establish hospitals, churches, comfortable quarters, clubhouses and schools, and to provide for the administration of Civil Law. The expenditure of a half billion dollars by the United States government was a cold business proposition. To be sure, the men in charge are happier when those working with them are happy, but individual interests can have no part in the administration of so great a work except as individual interests conduce and contribute to the effectiveness and expedition of the work to be accomplished.

The casual observer is apt to become so absorbed in the spectacular feats of the engineers as to be altogether oblivious to the no less important, though less evident, work of other departments. To him law and order, wholesome food, comfortable quarters and efficient sanitation are matters of course. He has them at home, and the very fact that he is comfortable and has a feeling of security while on the Canal Zone renders him oblivious to the basal conditions which make possible the rapid material progress everywhere so evident, so overwhelming. If these things were unsatisfactory, his attention would, of course, be forcibly called to them; since they are satisfactory, he does not notice them. After leaving the Isthmus the visitor will probably reflect that he saw seventy thousand people of every race and tongue behaving themselves in a manner not unlike that of his neighbors at home; that he saw policemen, dressed in neat brown khaki uniforms, in town and village, on trains and at railroad stations, enforcing order, not with club and pistol, but by their dignified though unobtrusive presence; that there must be courts of justice and the usual machinery incident thereto; that there were fire stations in each of the many Zone towns he visited; that he was told of a school system which furnished adequate facilities and tuition for the education of all children of whatever race and nationality; that his mail was delivered to him with as much expedition and in exactly the same way as it is delivered in the States; that he saw prisoners at work constructing macadamized roads for the government; that, on the whole, he found on the Zone a most cosmopolitan community of Americans, West Indians, East Indians, Chinese, Japanese, Spaniards, Turks, Syrians, Englishmen, Scotchmen, Frenchmen, Germans, Italians, Greeks, Scandinavians — all moving in a community where American ideas prevail and where American institutions obtain; and finally that while on the Zone he was so absorbed in the spectacular work of canal building that he did not acquaint himself at all with the very essential work of the Civil Government Department.

On April 9, 1904, Major General George W. Davis, U.S.A. (Retired), was appointed Governor of the Canal Zone and directed by the President to take formal possession of the Zone and the property of the United States therein and in the cities of Colon and Panama. A month later General Davis arrived on the Isthmus and immediately issued a proclamation announcing in the name of the President of the United States the occupation of the Zone territory by the American government. In evolving the present plan of organization a number of changes were made. The present Department of Civil Administration dates from January, 1908, from which time the department has been directed by the civilian members of the Commission, Jo. C. S. Blackburn (1907-1909) and his successor, M. H. Thatcher.

The Head of the Department of Civil Administration, in addition to such duties as he may be required to discharge as a member of the Isthmian Canal Commission, supervises the work of the various divisions of the department and all expenditures thereof, and represents the Commission and the Canal Zone government in their relations with the Republic of Panama and with the diplomatic and consular representatives of foreign countries accredited to Panama.

The executive work of the Department of Civil Administration comprehends the following civil divisions: —

> Posts, Customs and Revenues
> Police and Prisons
> Fire Protection
> Public Works
> Steam Vessel Inspection Service
> Schools
> Treasurer of the Canal Zone
> Auditor of the Canal Zone

The Judicial branch of the Department of Civil Administration includes the systems of Zone judiciary; namely, the Supreme Court, Circuit Courts and District Courts.

Division of Posts, Customs and Revenues

The Division of Posts, Customs and Revenues forms the Postal, Customs and Internal Revenue Service of the Zone. It also includes the collection of rentals from public lands and buildings, and the administration of estates. There are in the Zone sixteen post offices. All of these are money-order offices, and at all of them postal savings certificates are issued and deposits are received.

Under what is known as the Taft agreement, effective December 3, 1904, the Canal Zone government procures its postage stamps from the Panamanian government, paying the latter forty per cent of the face value of the stamps. The stamps are sold by the Division of Posts at their face value, and there is thus derived as net Zone postal revenues sixty per cent of the amounts realized on such sales. From this source the two governments realize, respectively, $48,000 and $32,000 annually. The total cost of administering the postal work of the Zone is about $160,000 a year, and the postal revenue is about $100,000 a year. Except for the amount paid the Republic of Panama for stamps, and the fact that so large a percentage of the mail handled is Commission mail and therefore franked, the Zone postal service would be self-sustaining.

The Customs work of this Division includes the entry and clearance of ships at the ports of Cristobal and Ancon, the signing and discharging of seamen, the enforcement of the collection of Panama tariff duties on importations coming into Zone ports, and the enforcement of the exclusion laws against Chinese and Syrians.

This Division also makes assessment and collection of taxes in the Zone. The tax scheme provides for the collection of a five per cent annual tax on the estimated rental value of lands and buildings held by private owners, for taxes on merchandise stocks, on polls of permanent residents, and for various license taxes. The collection of rentals on lands or buildings leased by the Commission is made by this division and the rentals become a part of Zone revenues. These revenues are applied to the construction and maintenance of roads and other public improvements in the Zone, to the maintenance of schools and to other local needs. The total of Zone revenues has been about $320,000 a year exclusive of postal receipts. The money-order sales have been more than five millions of dollars a year, the greater portion of which represents the savings of the employees of the Commission and of the Panama Railroad.

The head of this division serves under the title of Chief of the Division of Posts, Customs and Revenues. He is assisted in the work of the Division by deputy collectors and customs inspectors.

Division of Police and Prisons

The Division of Police and Prisons is under the immediate supervision of a Chief of Police. There are also an Assistant Chief of Police, two Inspectors of Police, three Lieutenants, eight Sergeants, fifteen Corporals, one hundred twenty-two white policemen and ninety negro policemen. The white policemen are usually ex-service men of the United States Army, Navy and Marine corps, many of whom have had military service in Cuba and in the Philippines; the black policemen are ex-members of the West Indian constabulary or of the West Indian Armies.

There is a Zone penitentiary in which are kept about one hundred forty convicts, most of them black, and these are employed in the construction of macadam roads in the Zone. There are police stations and district jails at the principal Zone points, and in the jails are kept the prisoners awaiting trial, and those who are serving sentences for the commission of misdemeanor offenses. The last named

I. SQUAD OF CANAL ZONE MOUNTED POLICE
II. A QUARTERMASTER'S CORRAL

prisoners are required to work in the maintenance of roads and streets. In the penitentiary a system of grading became effective February 24, 1911, whereby prisoners may, by good conduct, pass from the striped clothing grade to that of plain gray clothing. By this and other humane features, infractions of prison discipline have been greatly reduced, and the best prison results secured. Corporal punishment in the prisons is not tolerated.

Division of Fire Protection

The Division of Fire Protection is under the direct supervision of a Fire Chief. There are an Assistant Fire Chief, seven Captains, seven Lieutenants, forty-one Firemen, one Engineer, one Electrician, and one Lineman, all of whom are men of experience and have seen fire service in cities of the United States. At Cristobal, Gatun, Gorgona, Empire, Culebra and Ancon there are maintained fire stations with fire wagons, horses and the requisite force of firemen; and at the Cristobal and Ancon fire stations there are also automobile fire engines. In the smaller towns there are one-man fire stations, each in charge of a paid fireman, with hose wagon and hose; and at such points there are also maintained volunteer fire companies made up of Commission and Panama Railroad employees who turn out under the direction of the paid fireman and engage in fire fighting when fires occur. The work of this division has been especially efficient, as is evidenced by the small number of destructive fires in the Zone, notwithstanding the presence of so vast an amount of inflammable property.

Division of Public Works

The Division of Public Works is in immediate charge of a Superintendent of Public Works. This division performs for the Department of Civil Administration the work of maintaining the water, sewer and street systems of the cities of Panama and Colon, and makes collection of water rentals from private consumers in the two cities. These sanitary improvements are thus maintained agreeably to Treaty provisions. The water rentals are collected and are applied to the extinction of the debt due from the Republic of Panama to the United States government for the construction of these improvements in the two cities. Such construction was necessary to make these cities sanitary and wholesome, and in fifty years the improvements will have been fully paid for by the Panamanian government through the collection of water rentals from private consumers, and without cost to that government. The ownership of these improvements will then pass to the Republic of Panama.

This division also has charge of and rents out the markets owned by the Canal Zone government in the various Zone towns. These markets have been constructed in order to provide sanitary places for the sale of fruits, meats, vegetables and other articles. The revenues derived from such rentals are turned into the Zone Treasury.

One of Panama's greatest needs is good roads, and the splendid roads maintained by the Zone government furnish to Latin America an object lesson as to the value of such thoroughfares. The Panamanian government has already taken the cue and is now engaged in the construction of good roads between its more populous communities.

Steam Vessel Inspection Service

The Steam Vessel Inspection Service is directed by a Board of Inspectors who are required to inspect all vessels which come into Zone waters except those which have been duly inspected and certificated by the principal maritime governments.

The duties of the Treasurer and the Auditor of the Canal Zone government are such as obtain in positions of like character in the States.

Judicial Division

The Judicial Branch of the Department of Civil Administration is constituted as follows: four District Courts, three Circuit Courts and a Supreme Court. The Zone is divided into four administrative districts; in each there is a District Court with jurisdiction to try misdemeanors and minor civil cases, and with power to hold preliminary examinations of persons charged with felonies. The organization provides for five District Judges, one of whom is styled the Senior District Judge; and for three Circuit Court Judges who have jurisdiction of the more important misdemeanor cases, of felony prosecutions and of the more important civil litigation.

The Supreme Court is the final court of appeal in the Zone, and the three Circuit Judges sitting *en banc* constitute this court. Two of the Circuit Judges may, however, constitute a quorum, and this is usually necessary, as the appeal to be tried is usually from one of the three Circuit Judges. If, on such appeal, the two judges hearing it disagree, the appeal is lost; if they agree to reverse, a reversal is had, or if they agree to affirm, an affirmance is had. From the decision of this court there is no appeal. This fact has proved an advantage, because it would be quite difficult for defendants and litigants in the Canal Zone to prosecute appeals from the Supreme Court of the Zone to the courts of the United States.

Division of Schools

Ask any schoolboy what he is doing here and he will tell you "Helpin' to dig the big ditch." He has told more truth than he knows. The fact that it is possible for him to be here in good health, surrounded by a wholesome social atmosphere, and furnished with excellent school facilities, has made it easy for the Commission to secure the services of his father, who is an expert workman with serious intentions and fixed purposes.

The schools were organized into a system in 1906 and have steadily grown, until at present the system includes a Superintendent, two Assistants, a Music Supervisor, a Medical Examiner, eighty teachers and three thousand pupils. The schools are supported by revenues raised on the Canal Zone and are not an expense to the United States government.

The school buildings are constructed on the most recent plans evolved by scientific study in school hygiene, and are especially adapted to the tropics. They are equipped with modern sanitary steel desks and all the furnishings of the best graded systems of the schools of the States. Free texts, free stationery, free medical treatment and free tuition are furnished all children resident on the Canal Zone and all nonresident employees' children.

The qualifications required for appointment to

this division are high. No teacher in the United States can hope to get a position on the Canal Zone who has not had four years' high school training, at least two years' university or normal training and two years' successful teaching experience. It will thus be seen that the qualifications required are much above those of the average American city system. Politics and the recommendations of politicians have no place in the administration of the Canal Zone schools. The personnel of the Division of Schools is quite equal to that of the very best systems, and the organization, methods of teaching and equipment are such that men with families do not count inadequate school facilities among the objectionable features of living in Panama.

The small size of many of the communities has made the proper grading of the schools a difficult problem. As in the United States, free transportation was found to be the only remedy. In 1910 and 1911, a number of the white schools were consolidated. Children are transported by school wagons from the smaller to the larger towns. Children living in communities not connected with the larger communities by good roads are transported by rail. Hence a well graded system of schools is practicable.

A feature of the work of this division is its policy of giving practical education to the natives and to the West Indians. To accomplish this purpose,

SCHOOL GARDEN AT EMPIRE

I. PRIMARY GRADES AT PLAY, GATUN WHITE SCHOOL
II. NATIVE SCHOOL, SAN MIGUEL (148)

school gardens have been established at various places along the canal line. Notable among these is the school garden at Empire, where a thorough and systematic course in horticulture is given. Here bananas, papayas, cacao, okra, beans, peas, radishes, turnips, cabbage, lettuce, tomatoes and yams are cultivated with good results. While it requires considerable expense to produce crops indigenous to the temperate zone, the results achieved have been gratifying. All kinds of tropical fruits and vegetables do well here, and the coconuts, bananas, lemons, oranges, mangoes, alligator pears and pineapples are equal in size and quality to those grown anywhere. As the West Indian and native children will be dependent on the products of the soil for a livelihood, the practical training received will be invaluable.

The schools of the Canal Zone are in two divisions, the white and the colored. The white schools are attended by American pupils and taught by American teachers. The colored schools are attended by natives and West Indians, and are taught by West Indian teachers. So far as discipline, school equipment and methods are concerned, it may be said that the colored schools of the Canal Zone are much above the average schools of this type. The colored teachers are men who have graduated in the best West Indian colleges and who have had ample teaching experience in West Indian schools.

CHAPTER XI

OTHER DEPARTMENTS

OTHER departments whose work, though none the less important, is not quite so much in evidence to the visitor are the Departments of Law, Disbursements, Examination of Accounts, General Purchasing Office and Investigations, and the *Canal Record*. The relation of these departments to the general organization is shown on page 99.

The organization of the Department of Law comprises a Counsel and Chief Attorney for the Commission and the Panama Railroad Company, a Land Office and the Office of Prosecuting Attorney. The head of this department is the legal adviser of the Commission and the Panama Railroad. To quote from the annual report of 1911, "The head of this department has the direction and control of all litigation before the courts of the Canal Zone and the Republic of Panama in which the Commission or the Government of the Canal Zone or any of its dependencies are interested or involved, and the supervision and direction of all prosecutions of offenses against the laws of the Canal Zone."

In addition to these duties, the department drafts legislative measures for the Canal Zone government and has under its direction the execution of leases of public land, and the settlement of all damage claims arising from the invasion of private lands on the Zone on account of canal construction operations.

The majority of damage claims have arisen from the flooding of the Lake district by the impounding of the Chagres River at Gatun. This district comprises an area of one hundred sixty-four square miles, and all persons who have been able to establish reasonable claims to property therein have been liberally reimbursed for their losses.

Criminal and civil cases on the Canal Zone are handled by the courts in exactly the same way as such cases are dealt with in the States, except that all cases are presented by indictment, the Prosecuting Attorney prosecuting all felony cases. Minor offenses are tried in the District Courts upon presentation by police officers, but appeal may be had to the Circuit, and finally to the Supreme Court of the Canal Zone. The District Courts may be compared to the Justice of the Peace Courts in the States. Most of the criminal cases in the courts are brought against West Indian negroes and Spanish laborers. To the credit of Americans on the Zone, it is stated by Judge Frank Feuille, that "No colony of Americans anywhere under the flag presents a better record for law and order than that found among the Americans who are engaged in the work of building the canal."

The Department of Examination of Accounts, as the name implies, audits the financial transactions of all the departments. It does the bookkeeping of this big organization. Other duties fall to the office of the Examiner of Accounts, such as the checking of the various time keeping offices and the direction of the time inspection work.

One gets an idea of the stupendous nature of the work going on here from a glance at the table opposite, made up by the head of this department, showing a classified list of expenditures to February 29, 1912.

Under the direction of the General Purchasing Officer and Chief of Office at Washington are the following divisions: General Office, Disbursing Office, Office of Assistant Examiner of Accounts, Appointment Division, Correspondence and Record Division and Purchasing Division. The duties of this office may be summed up as follows: the advertising and letting of bids for all Commission supplies, through Assistant Purchasing Officers at New York, New Orleans and San Francisco; the selection and appointment of employees on the Isthmus; the consideration and settlement of contract bills against the Commission, the auditing of all receipts and disbursements made by the office, the inspection of

CLASSIFIED EXPENDITURES

Periods	Department of Civil Administration	Department of Law	Department of Sanitation	Department of Construction and Engineering	General Items	Fortifications	Total
To June 30, 1909	3,427,090.29		9,673,539.28	69,622,561.42	78,022,606.10		160,745,797.09
Fiscal year, 1910	709,351.37		1,803,040.95	26,300,167.05	2,863,088.83		31,675,648.20
Fiscal year, 1911	755,079.44		1,717,792.62	27,477,778.19	3,097,959.72		33,048,607.97
July, 1911	72,895.22	2,527.35	137,635.83	2,089,361.82	312,920.11		2,615,340.33
August, 1911	74,768.45	1,878.27	156,054.79	2,287,506.30	355,087.42	86,243.14	2,962,438.37
September, 1911	64,905.24	1,805.83	146,912.23	2,212,702.66	234,233.58	86,275.56	2,746,835.10
October, 1911	64,143.49	1,586.71	152,252.71	2,751,377.24	323,154.80	32,061.45	3,324,576.40
November, 1911	66,491.92	2,502.39	138,404.22	2,346,719.44	200,614.00	93,952.56	2,848,684.53
December, 1911	66,013.49	1,854.62	143,745.59	2,467,291.16	316,891.32	60,794.07	3,056,590.25
January, 1912	74,737.19	2,581.53	114,637.59	2,228,910.21	451,899.54	148,983.75	3,021,749.81
February, 1912	71,769.71	2,330.07	115,308.91	2,326,058.48	249,658.11	73,488.96	2,838,614.24
Total	5,447,245.81	17,066.77	14,300,224.72	142,110,431.97	86,428,113.53	581,799.49	248,884,882.29

all supplies forwarded to the Isthmus on government contracts, and arrangement of transportation for both new employees and those returning to the Isthmus from leave.

The Department of Disbursements has the custody of all Commission funds on the Isthmus. It has besides its money responsibility the issuance of all hotel and commissary coupon books to the various departments, and the receipt and expenditure of the appropriations for all phases of the construction work. The financial responsibility of this and of the Washington office is about $37,000,000 a year.

Besides the duties devolving upon him in keeping a record of the proceedings of the Canal Commission, the Secretary of the Commission investigates all complaints made by laborers to the Chairman of the Commission, and compiles and edits the *Canal Record*, the official organ of the Commission.

The *Canal Record* is published weekly, and is issued to all employees of the Government here. In its issues are the Chairman's monthly reports to the Secretary of War, notes on the progress and construction of the canal, personal notes of consequence, and official announcements and circular letters. The *Record* is strictly a business institution and as such perpetrates no funny pages, uses no superlative adjectives, reproduces no elegiac poetry, but deports itself along sober lines generally.

After our trip across the Isthmus it is unnecessary to discuss further the work of the Engineering Department. At the head of this department is the Chief Engineer. There are under his immediate direction the Atlantic, Central and Pacific divisions. In the office of the Chief Engineer are three divisions having charge of (1) masonry, lock structure, lock machinery, etc.; (2) meteorology, river hydraulics, etc.; (3) estimates, allotments of funds, rates of pay, cost keeping, etc. The Engineering Department is, as the French put it, the *raison d'être* of all the other departments.

PART TWO

THE CANAL COUNTRY

CHAPTER I

COLUMBUS

THE stirring scenes along the line of the canal are apt to make the tourist forget that he is in a land with a past. Yet the Isthmus of Panama is the birthplace of American history. When the Panama Canal is completed, the dreams of Columbus will have been fulfilled in the establishment of a New Route to India — the route which he sought in his first voyage into unknown western waters and which was to the end the object of his quest. Every schoolboy knows the absorbing history of this famous old navigator, who, because he had the courage of his convictions, braved superstition, prejudice and ridicule to launch into unexplored seas. But few realize the intimate connection which the Genoese sailor-hero has with the history of Panama and the canal. It is this part of the Columbus story which we must review in telling the story of Panama.

The discovery of America was an accident. The voyages of Columbus were actuated not so much by a desire to prove that the earth is round as to find the land of the Great Khan of China, that wonderful land abounding in riches — a land of spices, silks and manifold luxuries; a land whose glories Columbus had learned from Marco Polo and other overland travelers to the Orient. Now, among the things which incited Columbus on his westward voyage was Toscanelli's map, which showed the earth to be round but very small. According to Toscanelli's geography Asia and Europe occupied about two thirds of the globe's surface. So the east coast of Asia appeared on the map just about where America actually is. Small wonder, then, that Columbus, when he discovered the New World, refused to believe that the land he beheld was any other than that of Cipango and Cathay — Japan and China.

In all, Columbus made four voyages to America, but he died without knowing that he had discovered a new world, and with the firm conviction that very soon the "Secret of the Strait" would be solved and ships from Europe would sail into a leading port of the Orient. He believed he had found the new route to India. His fourth and last voyage was still in quest of this passage, which he felt sure would lead him directly to the throne of the Great Khan, to whom he carried letters of greeting from the monarchs of Spain. It was on this voyage that he discovered the mainland of the Isthmus of Panama. The pioneer of the New World thought of this newly

CHRISTOPHER COLUMBUS (161)
From a painting by Del Piombo, property of the Metropolitan Museum of Art.

discovered land as merely a part of the realms of Cathay. It remained for Balboa, some seven years later, to discover the existence of an isthmus and of another great ocean.

"In this same year, 1502, Christopher Columbus entered the fourth time into his discovery, with four ships, at the command of Don Ferdinand, to seek the strait which, as they said, did divide the land from the other side." Thus quaintly does the old Spanish historian, Galvano, introduce his tale of Columbus's fourth voyage by telling the one great motive which actuated the discoverer. Following the story, we find that Columbus on this voyage skirted the islands of Haiti and Jamaica and thence sailed westward past Cuba to Honduras Bay.

Now from the Bay of Honduras the coast line runs almost due east, and it was in this direction that Columbus, with his four flat-bottomed, clumsy boats, crept along against the wind. At last they reached the point where the coast makes a sharp turn to the south, and rounding it, found themselves pushed along by a welcome breeze from the north. Then in gratitude to the Almighty they named the point where their luck changed, "*Gracias á Dios.*" Down that shore line, famed in after years as the Mosquito Coast, thence along the Costa Rican shore and into the Chiriqui Lagoon, sailed Columbus. He had now reached the coast line of Panama, and he explored with care each river mouth and bay. He entered the River of Crocodiles, later the famous Chagres. Stopping at the Isle of Bastimentos — Isle of Victuals, so named by Columbus because the ships were provisioned there — the four vessels on November 2, 1502, entered the spacious deep-water harbor at Porto Bello, where he stayed for a few days.

Doubling back on his course Columbus again sought the entrance to the strait which he believed to exist along the Panamanian shore, for the Indians had told him that there was a narrow place between two seas; very likely the Indians meant the Isthmus. Spending the winter along the coast of Veraguas, the old admiral once more sought the strait, cruising south to the Gulf of Darien, where the Isthmus joins the mainland of South America. Giving up the quest here, he finally returned to Haiti.

Inasmuch as November 2 is the day of the month on which Columbus landed upon Isthmian soil and November 3 is the day now celebrated by Panamanian citizens as Independence Day, it has been suggested that the celebration be a double one, commemorating the discovery of the Isthmus and the freedom of the Republic. This would perhaps be appropriate were November 2, 1502, the actual date of the discovery, but it is not.

Columbus was not the discoverer of the Isthmus

of Panama. Preceding him by more than a year came Roderigo de Bastidas, who had set out from Spain in 1500, sailing directly for the Isthmian mainland. He made harbor at Porto Bello, and was perhaps the first European to touch Panamanian shores. Bastidas was, as were other explorers of the time, searching for the secret strait, so his visit fits in with the conceit that the early discoverers of the Isthmus were fathers of the modern canal idea. Since Bastidas landed at Porto Bello early in 1501, his discovery precedes that of Columbus by a good year and a half. He sailed thence southward to the Gulf of Darien and doubled back northward to Haiti. Bastidas had two motives for his voyage; he wanted to find the supposed strait, and he wanted to find gold. Later he made a second voyage, which was purely a gold-seeking expedition.

Following Bastidas and Columbus in their discoveries along the Isthmian coast, comes Alfonzo de Ojeda, but his story is so closely associated with the fascinating tale of Balboa that it had better be told in that connection. Ojeda had even preceded Bastidas in a visit to the western shore line of the Caribbean, but he probably did not go as far north as did Bastidas, who, the records tell, sailed northward into "nine degrees and two parts of the latitude." Ojeda sailed into the Gulf of Darien and along the coast of Venezuela.

Though we cannot give Columbus first honors in the matter of discovery along the Isthmian mainland, it is to the matchless Genoese navigator that the popular mind always turns when the discovery of America or of any part of it is mentioned. In Panama as elsewhere this is as it should be, for that intrepid sail into unknown seas in 1492 is directly responsible for all that followed. Though Bastidas did visit Porto Bello a year sooner, Columbus was the pioneer; and the statue erected to his memory stands most fittingly at the entrance of the great canal which is to materialize his dream of a direct route to Asia.

When the tourist lands and, as he is sure to do shortly afterward, whirls up palm lined Roosevelt Avenue and around the "point," he will come full upon one more striking reminder of the great Genoese — the life-size bronze statue of Columbus and the Indian Maiden, which, on its ten-foot pedestal of marble, overlooks the entrance to the canal through which some day will pass the commerce of the world. The statue (see frontispiece) was cast at Turin, Italy, for the Empress Eugenie, and was a gift from her to the Republic of Colombia in 1868. Two years later it was erected on an improvised base in the railroad yards in Colon as a part of the celebration attending the placing of the first cable there, which established telegraphic communication with the world. In 1877, when Count de Lesseps arrived, he had the statue removed from the railroad yards to the beautiful village of Cristobal, which he was building on the point of Manzanillo Island. The statue was placed in front of the Count's palace. Could the bronze eyes see, what emotions would the present activities inspire! At last, the New Route to India!

CHAPTER II

BALBOA

If there is any one figure among the brilliant array of Spanish explorers in the early part of the sixteenth century who stands out preëminently as the Isthmian hero, it is Vasco Nuñez de Balboa. His greatest exploit, the discovery of the Pacific, though told with meagerness of detail in the history books, makes a vivid appeal to the mind of the average school boy. Yet this event was only the crowning one of a career more interesting than any fiction. Cruel he was, but not more cruel than the standards of his time sanctioned, while his other shortcomings are lost sight of in the light of the dramatic events which brought about his untimely death.

Balboa was a nobleman of Spain and a soldier of fortune, who like scores of others had come out to the New World to seek adventures and to replenish his fortunes. He was with Bastidas when that explorer landed at Porto Bello, a year in advance of Columbus. When they had returned to Haiti, and the varying fortunes of those stirring days had resulted in the arrest of Bastidas, Balboa found himself without an occupation and decided to settle down as a farmer. But agriculture was little to the liking of such a rover, nor could he make a success of it. His debts overwhelmed him; finally he concluded that his only chance to escape from all his troubles was to conceal himself in a cask and to allow himself to be carried on board one of the vessels which lay in the harbor at San Domingo.

His scheme was successful. It so happened that the ship onto which he was carried was one of Encisco's, bound on a relief expedition to the Gulf of Darien where Ojeda and Niqueza had attempted to plant colonies. Once at sea Balboa made himself known, and overcame Encisco's determination to throw him overboard by telling of his previous trip to the Isthmian mainland with Bastidas and by promising to be of some service. He was a man of thirty-five, full of vigor, and with a knowledge of the mainland which Encisco wisely considered might make him worth having.

The expedition on which Balboa found himself followed up the ill-fated one of the year before, 1509, which had been undertaken by Ojeda and Niqueza. They had been appointed governors of all the mainland from Cape de la Vela on the Venezuelan coast to Cape Gracias á Dios off Honduras. With the Gulf of Darien as the dividing line between them, this whole country had been placed under these two governors. With four ships and three hundred soldiers Ojeda had preceded Niqueza on the trip to their provinces. Niqueza, who had followed with seven ships and eight hundred men, found Ojeda near Cartagena, weakened by an Indian attack and about to give up. Uniting forces, the two governors avenged themselves on the Indians. Then they founded several towns, among them Nombre de Dios.

This place, the oldest historic spot on that part of the Isthmus of interest to us, was so named by Niqueza after a shipwreck had scattered his men along the coast. Gathering them up and doubling Manzanillo Point, he came suddenly upon the harbor, and said, "Here we will land, in the name of God." Trusting to the Almighty to make up for the deficiencies of the spot, he established Nombre de Dios, which, despite its poor harbor and its unhealthful site, remained the chief Spanish port of the Atlantic side of the Isthmus during three-quarters of a century. Niqueza and Ojeda both perished in these enterprises, leaving the colony on the Gulf of Darien in charge of Pizarro, later destined to play a more important rôle in the drama of discovery and conquest.

When Encisco and Balboa arrived in 1510, they found the town of San Sebastian all but destroyed and the future conqueror of Peru ready to give up in despair. Then it was that Balboa proved himself to be a man of affairs. He had Encisco declared governor as the successor of Niqueza, and with him established the town of Santa Maria del Antigua on the west coast of the Gulf of Darien, opposite the site of San Sebastian. Of this new town, Balboa was made *alcalde* or mayor. Speedily on the heels of this, he quarreled with Encisco, gained the ascendancy, clapped that worthy into chains, and sent him back to Spain. This left the adventurer, who had started out a few months before in a cask, the chief power in all the Castilla del Oro country. A commission from Haiti strengthened his position, and he became the governor in name as well as in fact.

Balboa was now at the height of his power, making treaties with the Indians, sending Pizarro on exploring expeditions, and fighting the chieftains who opposed his progress. As Rolfe did in later years, he married a native Indian princess. He made an alliance with Comogre, a powerful chieftain. He made a trip up the Atrato River in search of a city of gold which the Indians said existed there. It was probably a tradition of the wealth of the Incas which had filtered through to the coast.

Only one cloud hung over the success of Balboa. It was the fear that the king of Spain might not relish his treatment of Encisco. Indeed, that monarch had sent word for Balboa to come home and answer charges. To checkmate this, perhaps, by doing some spectacular deed which would render his services on the mainland invaluable, he planned his great exploring trip to find the "South Sea" of which the Indians had told him.

On September 1, 1513, with one hundred and ninety white men, one hundred Indians and some savage dogs, Balboa left Santa Maria, his settlement on the Gulf of Darien. On September 8 he started inland. Hewing a path through the jungle, climbing mountains and fighting Indians, was slow work, so the party only made a few miles a day. At last, on September 25, from the top of a mountain in the Caledonian part of the Isthmus, the Spaniards sighted the Pacific. The first white men to look upon its mighty waters and to discover that Panama was only a narrow neck of land between two great seas, Balboa and his followers fell on their knees as their priest intoned a *Te Deum*.

Four days later, after more hewing through tropical undergrowth, Balboa waded into the waters of the "South Sea" and, brandishing his sword, proclaimed all the lands which its waters touched as belonging to the king of Spain — a mighty claim indeed, and one whose magnitude neither Balboa nor any one else of his time realized.

From Santa Maria, Balboa had crossed the Isthmus along what was afterwards surveyed as one of

BALBOA DISCOVERING THE PACIFIC OCEAN

(173)

the possible canal routes, the Caledonian route, which has the distinction of being the very shortest, though not the most feasible because of its elevation. Had he been armed with instruments, as was Lieutenant Wyse more than three centuries later, the explorer would have found the distance in a straight line from ocean to ocean only 31.8 miles. Floundering through rank vegetation and mountain fastnesses, Balboa traveled much farther than this to reach his goal.

A devout Catholic, Balboa named the bay into which he waded the Gulf of San Miguel, in honor of St. Michael, the saint whom his church celebrates on September 29. This name the gulf still bears. Balboa did not land in the Bay of Panama as Isthmian tourists are sometimes made to believe, nor did he cross the Isthmus within seventy-five miles of the present canal route. Visitors to Panama, and others long resident in the Canal Zone, climb a steep hill near Gorgona, called "Balboa Hill," thinking thereby to emulate the feat of the explorer. On a tree at its summit some one has placed a rude crosspiece which enthusiastic climbers declare must have been nailed there by Balboa himself. The hill is worth climbing, for from its top, on a clear day, one may get a view of both oceans; but it has no historic importance.

Determined to sail upon the sea into whose waters he had waded, Balboa constructed some rude boats and embarked, exploring the shores of the Gulf of San Miguel, and according to some accounts going as far as the Pearl Islands off the Bay of Panama. Returning, he brought rich stores of gold, silver and pearls. Arriving at Santa Maria with the consciousness of a deed well done, the discoverer sent the news to his monarch, who promptly concluded that Balboa had no time to come to Spain to answer Encisco's charges.

The king accordingly made Balboa governor of the newly discovered "South Sea" and of the coasts which it touched. Unfortunately for Balboa, the ship which bore him this good news brought out Pedro Arias de Avila, known in history as Pedrarias, who was to supersede the discoverer of the Pacific as governor of Castilla del Oro.

In the spring of 1514, Pedrarias, with his wife, seven ships and fifteen hundred men, arrived in Darien. Of his atrocious cruelties enough has been written to make him infamous. Summing up his character from a modern view, Johnson says, "The best thing about him was his old age, which made his days comparatively few in the land which he cursed." This is a mild criticism as compared with those made by the old historians who were contemporary with Pedrarias, not one of whom tries to defend him.

At once there was bad blood between Pedrarias and Balboa. Aside from the jealousy of Pedrarias, accounts differ as to the cause of the trouble. It is related that Pedrarias became the father-in-law of Balboa and that this led to domestic troubles. Again, it is said that Balboa refused to repudiate his Indian wife and marry the daughter of Pedrarias. At all events, there was hard feeling, and the situation boded no good for Balboa.

Immediately upon his arrival the new governor had arrested Balboa, but had been unable to convict him. Thereafter a truce was arranged between them; Pedrarias was to govern the Atlantic seaboard and Balboa was to be left free to continue his explorations on the "South Sea." For a long time Balboa had been revolving in his mind a scheme which he attempted to execute in 1516. Taking the materials for four ships, and utilizing the Indians to carry them across the almost impassable mountains, he launched in the Gulf of San Miguel the first ships to sail the Pacific. Undoubtedly his plan was to sail southward in search of the city of gold — a quest which Pizarro later realized in despoiling the Incas of Peru.

Putting back to shore because his crew had become frightened at the sight of a school of whales, Balboa was surprised by a company of soldiers under his old friend Pizarro, who had been sent out by Pedrarias to arrest him. The Isthmian hero was hurried back to Santa Maria, where a mere farce of a trial was held. He was convicted and, with Pedrarias hurling taunts at him from a near-by window, Balboa, at the age of forty-two, in the prime of a great career of discovery and exploration, was beheaded. He perished in 1517, four years after his discovery of the Pacific and when he was on the verge of an expedition to the south which might have been fraught with great achievements. It is interesting to note that the man who helped to bring about Balboa's untimely death was Pizarro, who was enabled by this judicial execution to carry out plans for which the credit belonged to Balboa.

Next to Columbus, the name of Balboa deserves, more than that of any other early *conquistador*, to be commemorated in modern Panama. A tardy recognition of this sixteenth century soldier of fortune has been recently made in changing the name of the Pacific entrance to the canal from La Boca to Balboa. In the future, when the ships of all nations cross the Isthmus through the man-made strait, they will pass at the Pacific gateway a port named after the intrepid explorer who first crossed the same Isthmus — the first civilized man to gaze upon the waters of the "South Sea."

CHAPTER III

THE ROYAL ROAD

FAST upon the heels of early exploration came the conquest and settlement of the Isthmus by the Spaniards. It was not, however, the kind of settlement which populates a land with people attached to the soil and interested in the development of natural resources. Indeed, the only attempts toward such development were made by cattle grazers on the plains of the Pacific coast and the logwood cutters of Campeche Bay, far north on the Isthmus of Tehuantepec in Mexico. It was the beginning of Spain's golden age in her colonies; no one had time to develop natural resources so long as wealth could be gathered by merely taking it away from the Indians.

So settlements here came to mean the establishment of towns, filled with merchants and connected by trade routes, along which might travel gold and silver captured by a Pizarro in Peru, or rich pearls taken by a Morales from the Pearl Islands in the Pacific. The amount of mineral wealth taken by Pizarro and his followers along the Pacific coast would be hard to comprehend even in this era of great fortunes. For a century and more it flowed in a constant, steady stream across the Isthmus of Panama and into the coffers of Spain.

The sending of this vast wealth across the Isthmus meant the building of cities to serve as clearing houses and the establishing of a great road across the tropical jungle. It is of this royal trade road, its terminals and intermediate points — the first transcontinental highway in the western hemisphere — that we would speak. The tourist who visits Old Panama and makes more than a cursory inspection of the historic place may catch a glimpse of this old road. It is now overgrown with vegetation and loses itself amid jungle flora before one has followed it a hundred yards. Yet it is the remains of what was once the richest highway in the world.

At the Pacific terminus of this royal road stood the city of Panama, whose ruins still exist, five miles from the site of the present city of that name. The old city was founded in 1519 by Pedrarias, the judicial executioner of Balboa, two years after he had brought about the explorer's death. A son of Pedrarias was one of the original settlers of the place. It became the chief Spanish city in the New World, possibly excepting Cartagena; at the time of its destruction by Morgan it had a population of about thirty thousand. It was a beautiful place,

A GLIMPSE OF THE ROYAL ROAD

"MORGAN'S BRIDGE" ENTRANCE TO OLD PANAMA

with its seven thousand houses, most of them of carved native cedar and others of stone, erected in Moorish style. Of its stone monasteries and convents the most pretentious was the cathedral of St. Anastasius, a truly glorious building whose ruins still stand, a silent reminder in a tropical wilderness of the beauty of a former age.

Besides the royal storehouses, built of stone and made extra strong to house the king's gold, there were some two hundred merchants' warehouses, guarded constantly by slaves. In addition there were the stone stables of the king, where the mules were kept. On stated occasions these mules filed out in long trains, to the music of tinkling bells tied round their necks, their backs laden with rich plate destined as cargo for the king's ships which lay at anchor across the Isthmus on the Atlantic side.

The port of old Panama was bad for shipping because of the tide which changes the water front to a mile of wet black mud with each rise and fall. The harbor, however, was spacious enough for the largest ships to ride at ease. At one place in the bay an arm of the sea crept inland to a little creek which rose with the tides. Over this creek was a stone arch bridge across which ran the royal highway. This stone arch still stands, a striking example of the careful masonry which the Spaniards always employed, and a favorite mark for amateur photographers who visit the old ruins. Back of the city lay beautiful rolling plains of grass.

From the metropolitan city of Panama, the clearing house for Spanish treasures garnered in South America and along the Pacific coast, the royal road traversed rolling savannas or tropical jungle to Cruces, which lies at the highest navigable point on the Chagres River, and where during the days of Spanish glory there was a division of the king's highway. One branch led to Nombre de Dios (and later it went to Porto Bello); the other was by water down the river to where it empties into the Atlantic ocean. There stood Fort San Lorenzo and the village of Chagres.

Cruces, which went by the name of Venta Cruz during the days when it was a busy transfer station on the Isthmian trade route, lay on the west bank of the Chagres. Its two score of dwellings and half as many warehouses lay snug along the river bank, while directly back of them stood the tropical forest, impenetrable save where the royal trail to Nombre de Dios picked its marshy, boggy way.

At Cruces the Chagres River widened so that several of the large, flat-bottomed boats bound for Nombre de Dios via the river route past Lorenzo could ride at anchor easily. When the river was not a raging torrent, it was easier to transport wares

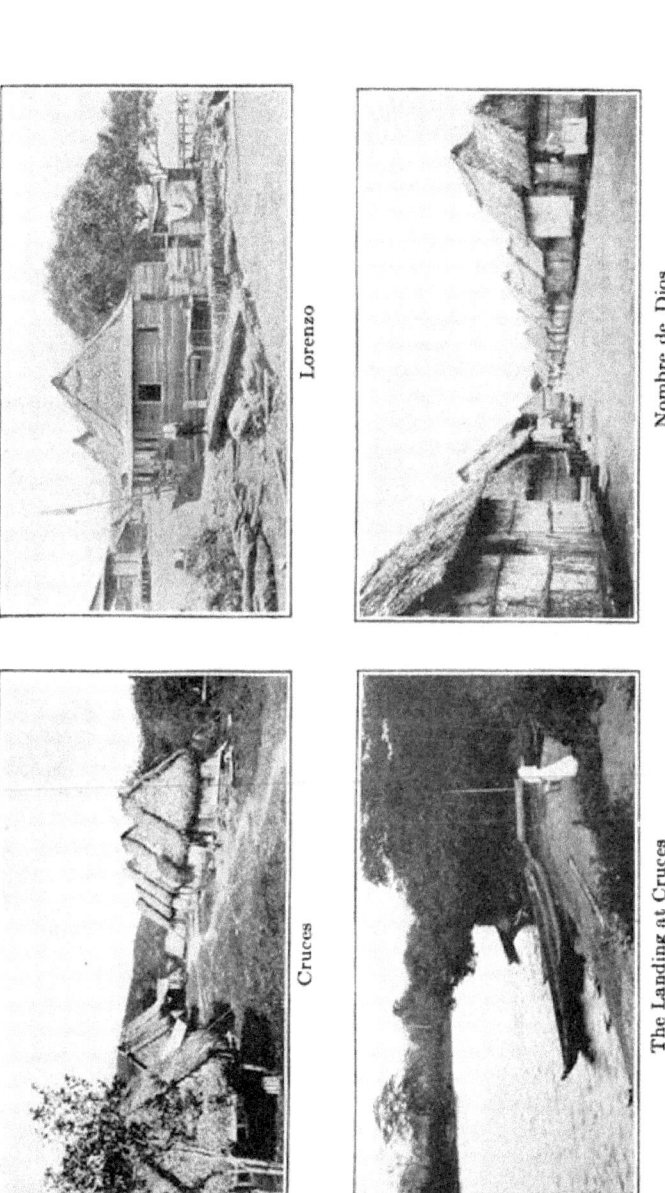

Cruces

Lorenzo

The Landing at Cruces

Nombre de Dios

HISTORIC VILLAGES AS THEY ARE TO-DAY

thus than to trust them to the mule trains which wormed their way across the trail from Cruces to Nombre de Dios and were always at the mercy of the Indians.

The stone structures of Cruces, besides the warehouses, were the official buildings and a large monastery with a church attached. The monastery was filled with friars and other religious persons, and the adjoining sanatorium with white women who came from Nombre de Dios to be delivered of their children. Modern Cruces gives little evidence of its former glory. It is a typical nondescript village of Latin America. The only visible remains of the one-time religious center are the three old monastery bells, which until recently stood in the open on a rudely erected standard and called the native worshipers to mass.

"San Lorenzo guards the Chagres entrance still," sings an Isthmian poet, and the almost literal truth of this cannot fail to impress the tourist who is so fortunate as to visit the well preserved battlements of this old fort at the summit of the mighty bluff which commands the entrance to the river. One needs but to see it to-day, two and a half centuries after its fall, to appreciate the feeling of security which the custodians of the king's wealth back at Cruces and farther back on the old highway in Panama itself, must have had in the knowledge that enemies of Spain must first pass Lorenzo to gain the river valley, the only easy means of access into the country.

Protected seaward by submerged rocks and offshore sand bars, the wall of natural rock rises a sheer one hundred feet from the water, both oceanward and riverward. From the land side it was made as nearly inaccessible as possible by an elaborate system of moats. At the crest of the bluff still stand walls of masonry, honeycombed with portholes. Inside is a solid causeway for cannon and passages which lead to underground dungeons. Even the old well is in a state of preservation which makes it worth seeing.

The castle stood on the seaward one of two peaks, the one to the landward being separated from the fort by a thirty-foot gully and connected by a drawbridge. In the days when it was a seat of Spanish strength, the masonry of the fort was reenforced with palisades and double fences of plank. Inside these were the thatched huts of the soldiers. Just below the fort, where the river bent inland, and a little above where the present native village stands, was the well protected port of Chagres.

Aside from Fort San Lorenzo, which served to protect the mouth of the Chagres River, the Atlantic termini of the Isthmian commercial highway were Nombre de Dios and Porto Bello. Of these two great shipping ports for Spanish wealth on the Atlantic side, Nombre de Dios was the older. Founded in 1510 by Niqueza, who after his vessels had been storm tossed gave the place its name by declaring he would land there "in the name of God," Nombre de Dios was never more than a makeshift of a place. Even in Niqueza's time the three sediment bearing streams which empty into its bay had rendered its harbor a poor one.

The bay was shallow, full of rocks, and open to the north winds, which often raised gales dangerous to shipping. During the two centuries that the place was abandoned, the streams carried down their sands and completely covered up the remains of the old town. When the Isthmian Canal Commission revived Nombre de Dios in 1908 by making it the source of the sand supply for lock and dam construction, the workmen dug up the hulks of two vessels. Frequent evidences of the sixteenth century importance of the place are unearthed.

Nombre de Dios was never a large place. A stretch of sandy beach, some sixty houses about a central square with streets crossing at right angles; directly back of this the tropical jungle, so close that the jaguars often came into town — this was Nombre de Dios, according to descriptions by those who saw it during its great days. The town was unwalled, though a gate stood where the royal road from Panama entered it. No more unhealthful spot could have been found along the Isthmian mainland. The fever raged the year round. The mortality among white children was very great. For this reason they were taken to Cruces, where there was a hospital and where the children were left until they had reached six years of age. Then they were thought old enough to stand the Nombre de Dios climate.

But if Nombre de Dios was a dull, monotonous place most of the time, for one month it was lively enough. Once each year a messenger came from Panama with news that the plate fleet from Peru had arrived there. A boat was immediately dispatched to Cartagena where the big fleet of Spanish galleons lay in wait to carry the treasure to Spain. By the time these ships hove in sight, Nombre de Dios was a changed place. Lodgings were crowded, tents and booths grew up in the plaza and in the streets. The city was filled with merchants, soldiers and pleasure seekers arriving in a constant stream from Panama, along with the mule trains of rich plate, precious stones and vicuna wool which came over the royal road to the tinkle of the bells. Until the merchants had disposed of their wares to the outgoing galleons a typical fair of the Middle Ages was on. As soon as the ships weighed anchor, Nombre de Dios was again almost depopulated.

Porto Bello, whose site was the first "firm-land"

along the Isthmian seaboard discovered by Columbus and Bastidas, became the great Atlantic terminus of the road in 1584, when a royal mandate was issued making it supersede Nombre de Dios on account of its superior harbor. It was not until almost the close of the century, however, that Nombre de Dios actually surrendered her glory to the new port, the delay being caused by the necessity of a change in the royal road, which meant the making of a new trail across the jungle between Cruces and Porto Bello.

The old town of Porto Bello stood on the southeastern side of what is perhaps the best natural harbor along the Atlantic seaboard of the American Isthmus. Its superiority over the harbor at Colon is in evidence every "dry season," when to escape the terrific "northers" the vessels lying at anchor in Limon Bay scurry to Porto Bello for safety. The shape of the harbor made the place easy to fortify, a fact which was taken advantage of by the Spaniards. On the western side of the harbor, a mile and a half across the bay from the town, stood Iron Castle, on an immense bluff. If ships sought to escape its fire by standing away toward the town on the opposite side, they were exposed to the guns of Castle Gloria and Fort Jeronimo.

Gloria, with its broad expanse on the water front and its upper and lower batteries, guarded the entrance to the city proper, while Jeronimo stood on a sand bank off Guinea town, that part of the city inhabited by slaves and negroes. All three of these old forts, though crumbling masses of ruin to-day, are well preserved in certain parts, and form an interesting modern commentary on the greatness of this city in the seventeenth century.

We must draw our picture of old Porto Bello from the scanty descriptions left by various buccaneers who sacked the place from time to time. The town nestled on a strip of narrow plain on the southern shore of the harbor, the hills rising most abruptly on all other sides. Indeed, the town was in a valley made pestilential by the vapors which poured down upon it from the surrounding mountains. The intense heat was not even relieved by the rainfall which deluges the place in the rainy season. It always gets more than its share of water during the wet period, a record of ten inches in one day being the high watermark there during December of 1908.

Porto Bello was a much more pretentious place than Nombre de Dios. In the western part of the city were stately stone churches, merchants' dwellings of fine cedar, the stone palace of the lieutenant general, a stone convent and a hospital. A great shipping port, the city centered its activities along the quay and the stone customhouse, past which and fronting on the bay ran the main street. From this

PORTO BELLO, SHOWING CANAL ZONE VILLAGE

OLD PORTO BELLO AS IT IS TO-DAY

(194)

ran the resident cross streets, leading to the two squares or plazas, on one of which faced the lieutenant general's establishment. There were perhaps one hundred fifty buildings in this part of the town. To the east, and separated from the aristocratic section by a small river, lay Guinea town. Like Nombre de Dios, Porto Bello's population increased tenfold once each year when the mule trains arrived from Panama.

Modern Porto Bello occupies the slope of that bluff where old Iron Castle once kept a stern vigil against pirates who might come to despoil the city across the bay. Its battlements no longer resound with cannonading, but with the booming of dynamite charges which tear loose the rocky steeps used in building the masonry of the Panama Canal. A modern rock-crushing plant occupies the hillside, while the ravine which one day furnished access to the old fort, is dotted with the trim cottages of an American Canal Zone village. Across the bay, about the ruins of the former city, are scattered the huts of a native village whose inhabitants little dream of the glory which once lay about them.

CHAPTER IV

SIR FRANCIS DRAKE

ANY account of Spain's glory in her Isthmian ports of the sixteenth century would be incomplete without the romantic tales of the English pirates who, long before Spain had reached the culmination of her golden era in the western hemisphere, became a menace to the rich galleons throughout the Spanish Main and to the wealth laden mule trains of the Isthmus. Beginning with Sir Francis Drake, we find a galaxy of brilliant adventurers whose bravery, quaint ideas of honor and personal honesty partly compensate for the evil of their calling. A good half dozen of the greatest ones, who followed in Sir Francis' footsteps — Parker, Morgan, Sharp, Ringrose, Wafer and Dampier — found the Isthmus the logical place for their principal operations.

While we cannot reconcile the careers of these knights of the mast and of the tropical Main with our modern standard of ethics, in all fairness to them it must be said that Spain brought much of their ravaging upon herself. Having settled at Santo Domingo in Haiti and in other ports of the West Indies, driving the Indians to the interior or

THE PANAMA TREE (197)

It was from this tree that the Isthmus of Panama received its name.

killing them off, as best suited her convenience, Spain had become firmly established, and regarded the country as her own. Accordingly she resented the peaceful visits of English, Dutch or French traders who came on some mission of commerce. This resentment grew into open hostility, and eventually into a state of war, which continued vigorously for a hundred and fifty years. Treaties of peace between the mother countries did not serve to lessen this enmity. A Spanish port or a Spanish galleon was considered legitimate prey by the rovers, while the rovers themselves, on a mission peaceful or piratical, were never safe from the Spaniards unless they came in overwhelming numbers.

The English achieved distinction as special objects of Spanish hatred, partly because of the sixteenth century strife between Spain and England, but largely because the English came in greater numbers than did the French and the Dutch adventurers. From this state of semilegitimate warfare, it was but a step to the buccaneering which Drake and his followers openly pursued, winked at, if not licensed, by the home government.

In 1563 Francis Drake, then a lad of eighteen, made a trading trip to the Spanish Main with his cousin, Sir John Hawkins. Forced to put in at Vera Cruz on account of a storm, the English had no sooner arrived than a Spanish squadron hove in sight. Fearing that they would be treated as pirates, Hawkins made plans to prevent the Spaniards from entering the harbor, and he might have been able to carry out his plans. The Spanish, however, insisted that they meant no harm. Finally they were allowed to enter, and then they treacherously attacked the English. Of the English fleet only two ships escaped, on one of which was Drake. This event Drake always gave as his reason for a lifelong hatred of the Spaniards. If, as it is claimed, Drake recorded an oath on this occasion to make the Spaniards "rue the day,' he certainly made them rue it during the subsequent quarter of a century in which he was a terror to every Spanish garrison from Trinidad to Campêche.

In 1572 Drake set out for the Spanish Main with two well equipped ships and seventy-three men. He was not only provisioned for a long stay, but well supplied with all the necessities for a freebooting expedition. It was characteristic of him that he should go prepared for emergencies. Information gained on previous voyages directed him to a secret haven along the Spanish Main from which he could work out what was perhaps the greatest Isthmian raid. The sack of Nombre de Dios, and the capture of the rich plate which was to go via mule train across the Isthmus to be unloaded on ships for Spain, were Drake's two objects.

About three o'clock one morning in the summer of 1572, Drake and his men, most of them youngsters, put into the harbor at Nombre in four small boats. Landing without accident, they spiked the few batteries of the place, and before the townspeople knew what was happening, had attacked Nombre de Dios and secured positions of vantage. Drake charged, the Spaniards fled pell-mell, and the pirates gathered at the governor's palace to seize the plate stored there and to break into the treasure house filled with precious pearls and gold. But all this took time, and Drake's men, being inexperienced, were almost as much confused by the novelty of it all as were the Spaniards. Then came a typical Nombre de Dios shower. It deluged everything, and considerably dampened the ardor of the English. Suddenly it was discovered that Drake was injured, and the pirates, now nearly in a panic, retreated to their boats with only a small part of the booty they could have captured.

Undismayed by this near-failure, Drake determined to make good the purpose of his expedition by capturing the Spanish plate on its way across the Royal Road. The plan was to go up the Chagres River to Cruces and waylay the treasure caravans *en route* from Panama to Nombre de Dios. This treasure, the annual shipment from Peru, was due to go over the Isthmian route about the first of the year, 1573. Becoming friendly with the Maroon Indians, Drake and his party made the trip to Cruces without incident. Accounts of this trip contrast strangely with the story Esquemeling tells of the hardships which Morgan's expedition underwent a century later. Drake, however, had certain advantages, chief of which was that he was stealing up the river valley unmolested by hostile natives.

Getting beyond Cruces and almost within sight of the rolling savannas of Panama city, Drake and his party awaited the treasure train. They even sent a spy into the city to learn the time the caravan was to start. But the indiscretion of a member of the Drake party spoiled all the well laid plans. He allowed himself to be seen by a Spanish horseman who, becoming suspicious, advised a ruse. The experiment of changing the order of the mules was made. Instead of sending in front the fourteen mules that were loaded with gold and jewels, they were shifted far to the rear, while the beasts that bore unimportant baggage were sent ahead.

The English fell upon the caravan when it first reached their ambush. This gave ample time for the rest of the caravan to make a safe retreat into Panama with the precious cargo. When the pandemonium following the sudden attack had subsided and the pirates had time to realize their mistake, they fell back upon Cruces and attacked it. But the warehouses of the place were almost empty and Drake got little out of the raid.

Disappointed again when untold wealth seemed almost within his grasp, Drake became desperate in his desire to make his expedition a success. The treasure caravan had yet to make the trip across the Isthmus, and the only thing left was to waylay it. Retreating from the Isthmus, Drake was successful, with the help of the Indians, in making it appear that he had left the Spanish Main for good.

Accepting as a partner Captain Tetu, a French pirate with twenty men, Drake with his own diminished force of thirty sneaked back into the Isthmus by way of the Francisco River. It was a long way to Nombre de Dios, but the adventurers managed to creep up unnoticed until they were almost within hailing distance of the town. They were just in time, for the mule trains were now coming along with bells tinkling; and their guardians had no thought of danger. With a sudden swoop, Drake's force fell upon the richly laden caravan. The thirty Spanish foot soldiers were overcome and the bulk of the treasure captured.

How much wealth the pirates took on this raid is not known, but an old chronicler puts it at "thirty tons of silver." In addition there were precious jewels and much gold. It would be safe, perhaps, to estimate the value of the booty at one hundred thousand dollars. Of course, they could not carry it all away, and much of it was buried, as it was necessary to beat a hasty retreat before the Spaniards could recover.

The sheer audacity of Drake's successful attempt is evident when it is remembered that he had scarcely more than half a hundred men and was many miles from his base. Captain Tetu, the French pirate, had been wounded, and it was necessary to leave him behind in the forest with two comrades to guard him. One of the men later escaped to tell a horrible story of how the Spaniards had captured them and had slain his two companions.

By the middle of the summer of 1573 Drake, with his two vessels heavy laden with spoils, was back in England. It was by no means his last voyage against the Spanish. He raided Nombre de Dios again in 1595, burning the town. It was at Nombre de Dios that Drake contracted the flux of which he died. Off the harbor at Porto Bello, which he sacked in 1595, following his final raid at Nombre de Dios, the old Admiral's body was lowered to rest in Davy Jones's locker, which has served as the tomb for so many adventurers of the Spanish Main.

CHAPTER V

MORGAN'S ISTHMIAN RAIDS

IF the Spaniards had cause to fear Sir Francis Drake during his activity along the Spanish Main, they also had occasion to recall him and to heap imprecations upon his memory during the century following his death. The success of his raids opened up new roads to power and to wealth for many an adventurous English sea-dog. For a century after Drake, preying upon Spanish commerce and Spanish ports in the New World became a recognized occupation.

The hazardous features of the life were offset by the prospect of enormous gain, while the adventure itself held strong attraction for the roving spirits of that day.

The term "buccaneer" was brought into the English language by these terrors of Spanish America. Leading a rough life when ashore, the pirates "boucanned" their meat after the manner of the Indians along the coast of Brazil; that is, they cured their fresh meat by placing it on a grating above their camp fires, smoking it with the fumes of burning green sticks. They ate the meat, thus cured, without further cooking.

The ports of the Isthmus of Panama were never free from danger during the hundred and fifty years when the pirates were operating in the New World. The menace became so great that for a time the Royal Road from Panama to Nombre de Dios and Porto Bello was almost abandoned, the vast wealth of Peru finding its way to Spain via the Strait of Magellan. But in 1579, Drake made his memorable voyage around the Horn and wrought such havoc upon Spanish galleons that commerce once more shifted to the Isthmian route as the less dangerous.

Of all the pirates who visited the Isthmus on missions of pillage after Drake's time, Henry Morgan is perhaps best known, partly because of the devastation he wrought and partly because of the interesting and detailed account which Esquemeling has left us. Morgan was a Welshman without means. In 1665 he joined with Mansvelt, a pirate of Dutch extraction, to colonize the island of Santa Katalina off the Nicaraguan coast as a rendezvous for buccaneers. Mansvelt died without completing the project, and the island was captured by a Spanish expedition under the governor of Panama. It is interesting to note that the English prisoners seized at the capture were taken to Porto Bello, where they were set to work in constructing Iron Castle, one of the strongholds which Morgan captured a few years later.

Morgan was in Jamaica at the time Santa Katalina fell and was not seriously handicapped by its loss. Indeed, he had gained so much prestige by his alliance with Mansvelt that shortly afterward he was able to lead a piratical expedition of twelve ships and seven hundred men, English and French, against the town of Puerto del Principe in Cuba. This was in 1665, ten years after Jamaica was seized by the English. The fact that the island now belonged to England meant much to Morgan and to subsequent freebooters. Unlike Drake, they were never too far from an operating base, and if it became necessary to have a show of authority for their operations, they could generally get a commission from the governor of Jamaica. It was on the pretense that the Spanish were intending to attack the island that Morgan now planned his raid against Porto Bello.

It was only four years less than a century after Drake's famous voyage against the Atlantic ports of the Isthmian trade-route, when Morgan set out with a fleet of nine sail and four hundred sixty military men to plunder Porto Bello. This was no small undertaking, to go against such a stronghold, nestled securely in its fort-girdled harbor, well garrisoned and only sixty miles from Panama, where there was a larger force.

Esquemeling tells the story of the sack of Porto Bello in form as accurate as we are able to get it. He was himself a pirate, probably Dutch; he was on the Morgan raids of 1668–1671, and he wrote his account seven years after. The pirates, according to Esquemeling, anchored their ships about ten leagues from the city, and then entered small boats. Going ashore some time after midnight, they came upon the outermost sentry, whom they bound securely, and plied with questions as to the strength of the garrison. Advancing toward the city the buccaneers came to an outlying castle, which they surrounded, and made demands for a quiet surrender. But the garrison opened fire, arousing the whole town.

The fort was easily taken. Morgan, perhaps incensed because it had not surrendered quietly, allowed his men to blow up the fort with all the Spaniards therein, after they had been assembled in one room for that purpose. By this time all Porto Bello was in an uproar. Soldiers hurried to the guns and battlements, excited citizens rushed to places of protection, pausing to cast their money and jewels into cisterns and wells. The governor was unable, because of the confusion, to rally his people, and so retired to one of the castles and began a steady fire on the pirates.

From this time on the battle was in deadly earnest

and lasted from break of day until noon. The attack centered about the castle in which the governor had taken his stand. Attempts to burn it were frustrated by the Spaniards, who threw down pots of burning metal upon the pirates. Attempts at scaling the walls were equally futile until Morgan adopted a most inhuman trick. Early in the struggle a number of nuns and friars had been seized. Hastily constructing some scaling ladders, Morgan's men forced these religious people to place them on the walls, expecting that the governor would not fire on his own people. He was mistaken, however, for the poor souls, while pushed forward by the pirates to place the ladders, were fired upon by their own people. They "sent their wails heavenward and died agonizing deaths." The scheme was successful. With the ladders so placed it was possible for the pirates to capture the castle, which meant the fall of the city. The bravery of the governor is extolled by Esquemeling, who says that he refused quarter and died defending the fort, despite the pleadings of his wife and his daughter. For fifteen days the pirates stayed at Porto Bello, sacking, reveling and engaging in all manner of excesses. Then Morgan demanded and received from the citizens a ransom of $125,000. The governor of Panama sent a small company of soldiers to the aid of Porto Bello, but they were driven back by the pirates at a pass outside the city. After that the Panama executive left the place to its fate.

The sack of Porto Bello completed, Morgan returned to the West Indies to live in rioting and debauchery. The wealth the pirates had seized did not last long, however, and inside two years Morgan found it necessary to get up another expedition. The success of his Porto Bello raid had given him a reputation, so he did not have to call twice for volunteers. Indeed, pirates from all over the Indies flocked to the Isle of Tortuga, which he had appointed as a rendezvous. Here, on October 24, 1670, Morgan was made admiral of an enormous expedition and drew up the terms of contract for one of the biggest raids ever attempted. There were thirty-seven ships and two thousand pirates.

At the head of such a force, Morgan was no longer a freebooting pirate without means or influence. He carried letters from the Jamaican government and gave his expedition the formality of legal sanction by furnishing each of his captains with letters which permitted them to capture any Spanish vessels on the high seas or to go against any Spanish port. In fact, some English writers choose to consider him the saviour of the English West Indies at this time. Morgan's position is in strong contrast with his position in the Porto Bello raid.

At the conference in Tortuga three places were

discussed as objective points for the raid — Vera Cruz, Cartagena and Old Panama. The last mentioned was finally chosen. On its way to the Isthmus the Morgan expedition stopped at the island of Santa Katalina which Mansvelt had planned to make a piratical stronghold a few years before. The place was now in the hands of the Spaniards, but with little difficulty Morgan's men captured it — the Spanish governor making a deal to surrender after a make-believe attack and defense which were arranged to deceive the Spanish governor at Panama. While the bulk of Morgan's expedition tarried at this island, Captain Brodley, one of his lieutenants, with four ships and four hundred men, set out to take Fort San Lorenzo at the mouth of the Chagres River.

It was a small expedition for so large an undertaking, and the wonder is how they ever managed to take that great natural stronghold. Morgan must have had great confidence in Brodley's ability, for Esquemeling says the expedition was "no larger lest the Spaniards should become aware of the later designs upon Panama." Had Brodley failed, the great raid against Panama would have been well-nigh impossible.

On the seaward side of Castle Chagre, or Fort San Lorenzo, is a ravine which separates the natural bluff of Lorenzo from the hill opposite. This ravine is about sixty feet deep and is the valley of a little stream which here trickles into the small bay at the east of the fort. It was on to this barren slope opposite Fort Lorenzo that Captain Brodley and his men suddenly pounced one afternoon. They had secreted their vessels down shore and crept upon the fort through the mangrove swamps.

Despite their attempts at surprise, the Spanish garrison was ready, and with cries of "Come on, you English heretics; you shall not get to Panama this bout," the Spaniards met the first charge of the pirates with a terrific fire. The stubborn defense compelled the English to retire into the jungle and to await the passing of daylight. Then the pirates renewed their attack; again and again Brodley's men rushed across the ravine under a withering fire from the fort. Almost a fourth of the pirates were dead and no headway had been made toward the capture of Chagre.

Finally, so the story goes, a pirate running across the ravine in a stooping posture was struck in the back with an arrow. Drawing it out, he wrapped its shaft with cotton for a wad, and placing it in his musket, shot it back over the wooden palings which formed the palisades of the fort. The cotton had ignited from the discharge of the gun. By the merest chance the blazing arrow struck in the vicinity of a palm thatch close to a powder magazine. Unnoticed by the Spaniards, the fire gained headway,

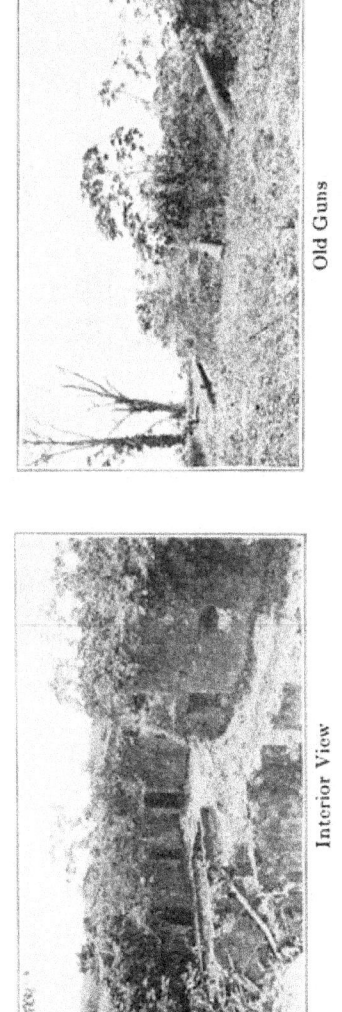

Interior View

Old Guns

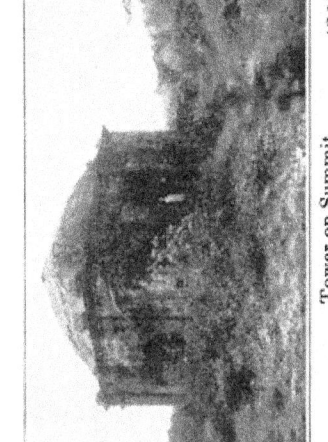

Entrance

Tower on Summit

FORT LORENZO OF TO-DAY

(213)

until a terrific explosion brought the garrison running to the scene. Thus the guns guarding the palisades were left unmanned and the pirates were able to set fire to the rows of wooden palings. The English then retired to the woods to watch the palisades burn. When the fire abated, the pirates saw that a perfect slope of earth ran from the bottom of the ravine to the top of the outer walls; by rushing up that slope they could reach the inside of the fort.

Until morning Brodley's men contented themselves with picking off Spanish soldiers who were exposed in the bright light of the blazing fort. The second day dawned with everything in favor of the English, but the brave Spanish garrison had not given up. Just as if the walls still protected them, the garrison maintained a steady fire from the guns. But by noon the vigor of the English attack began to tell; the last stand had been made at the inner castle on the top of the fort; the governor had been killed; all but forty of the garrison of three hundred and fourteen were dead; the pirates had lost more than a hundred killed and seventy wounded. Of the mere handful of Spaniards left alive, some eight or ten had slipped away to carry the news of English success up the Chagres River to Panama.

A few days later Morgan's main force from Santa Katalina hove in sight of Fort San Lorenzo. It is said that when the pirate fleet saw the English colors, their joy was so great that the crews of four of the ships allowed their vessels to drift on to the reef which runs out from the opposite bank of the river. A storm came up and the four ships were beaten to pieces on the coral beach. Most of their cargo was saved, however, and plans went on apace for the trip up the Chagres to Panama. Morgan rebuilt Fort Lorenzo, repaired the palisades, rethatched the huts, and left a garrison of five hundred pirates to hold the place as a base of operations while, with twelve hundred men, he started out on his memorable trip across the Isthmus. The start was made on January 18, 1671.

Of the hardships of this ten-day march across the Isthmus, Esquemeling has left us a graphic account. The pirates were unable to carry provisions, and since the Spaniards and Indians had devastated the country before them and had destroyed every source of food supply in sight, the English suffered the extreme of hunger and of thirst. A tropical jungle is repellent to human beings. How much of a death trap it must have seemed to the pirates, who stumbled ahead with the knowledge that hostile eyes might be peering at them from every bit of foliage and that the inhabitants of the country, both white men and red, considered them enemies whose death by starvation would be almost too easy a fate!

In a vivid picture Esquemeling convinces us that these ten days were days of terrible hardship. "The

Spaniards, being every one fled and leaving nothing behind them unless it was a small number of leather bags, our hunger grew so sharp that it did gnaw our very bowels." On the fifth day the pirates reached Barbacoas, on the seventh day Cruces and on the ninth they were fortunate enough to find some bread and wine in the storehouses belonging to the king. Most of them fell sick after eating and believed themselves poisoned. However, it was only the natural sickness following excess in eating after a forced period of fasting.

Coming upon the rolling green savannas before the royal city of Panama, the pirates saw a sudden end to their days of hunger. Without stopping to contemplate the beautiful picture of Old Panama nestled in her peaceful bay, they fell upon the grazing asses, cattle, and horses and satisfied their gnawing appetites. On the tenth day the buccaneers advanced toward Panama, whose possession was to be disputed with the flower of Spanish chivalry, consisting of four hundred horse and twenty-four hundred foot soldiers. In addition, the Spanish force included sixty Indians and negroes, who were to drive two thousand wild bulls into the English camp. This, according to Esquemeling, was the formidable force which the Spanish were able to line up against the tired buccaneers. The governor of Panama puts the number of foot soldiers at fourteen hundred and the horse at two hundred.

CHAPTER VI

PANAMA AND THE PIRATES

CERTAINLY the Spaniards were equal to the pirates in point of numbers and they had the added advantage of being on the defensive and of being near their base. However, instead of making the pirates do the attacking — which in their desperate state they would have been forced to do — the four hundred Spanish horse wheeled into battle and charged across a boggy field. Then, just as their English forbears had done when the French charged at Agincourt, the buccaneers put one knee to the ground and poured deadly volleys into the floundering horse. The rain of bullets on the savannas of Panama had the same effect as the shower of arrows at Agincourt. In two hours' time the Spanish attack had become a rout. The foot soldiers had been no more successful than those on horse, while the two thousand wild bulls became frightened with the noise of battle and ran away.

The pirates were too exhausted to follow the fleeing Spaniards, who sought refuge in the jungle which bordered the savannas. After a rest the buccaneers marched on the city, the way to which was now open. Some effort at defending it was made, so there were three hours of fighting before the whole place lay at the mercy of Morgan. A detachment of pirates was dispatched to round up the citizens in hiding. They brought in two hundred prisoners who were tortured into revealing the whereabouts of their treasure. In marked contrast to their wild excesses at Porto Bello, the buccaneers remained sober and went about their pillage and robbery in a very businesslike manner. Esquemeling says Morgan kept his men sober by pretending he had secret intelligence that the Spaniards had poisoned all the wine in the city.

This precaution was not effective throughout the pirates' stay, however, for the chroniclers tell of several instances of riotous excess by the invaders. At Taboga one party of them allowed a rich galleon to escape because they wanted to get some casks of fine wines which they had heard were on the island. Morgan, himself, did not live up to the code of morals he prescribed.

Three weeks the pirates held Panama city, or what was left of it, for shortly after the capture several of the important buildings caught fire. Despite the combined efforts of the pirates and citizens, nothing could stop the flames. In two days' time whole streets had burned out. Esquemeling attributes the fire to Morgan, though just why he should turn incendiary at this time is not clear. At the end of these memorable three weeks the pirates had stripped the city and had collected all the available ransom from the citizens. Morgan's threat to those who had been slow in paying their ransom was transportation to Jamaica as slaves.

On February 24, 1671, Morgan and his men departed from the ruins of the city which they had found at the height of commercial prosperity less than a month before. The pirates with their prisoners marched back along the same route over which they had come. At Cruces many of the prisoners were able to pay their ransom and were released. Arriving at Fort Lorenzo, Morgan had the spoil divided. Everybody was dissatisfied with the small share, about one hundred dollars, which was given to each man. It seemed a most inadequate amount after the hardships and dangers to which they had been exposed.

The expedition, after all, had not been very successful. Despite the vigor of the pirates' attack on Panama and their scouring of the seas in quest of treasure-laden ships, one galleon containing all the king's plate newly arrived from Peru had escaped. On board this boat were also the nuns of a certain monastery who had not forgotten to take with them all the rich ornaments of the church. In proportion to the devastation wrought and the hardships endured by the pirates, the raid on Panama was not as successful as that on Porto Bello.

The pirates felt they had good cause to curse Henry Morgan for his unfair division of the spoils, and they did not hesitate to curse him to his face during the few days' stay at Fort Lorenzo. At last, when the advice boat had returned from Porto Bello with a message from its citizens declaring they would do nothing toward ransoming the fort, the admiral judged it wise to steal away while he was still safe. Making secret preparations he sailed from Lorenzo, followed by only a few of his ships and without the formality of an adieu to the majority of his men, whom he left amidst the ruins of the old fort. The deserted pirates got away the best they could, financially but little better off than when they started on the hazardous expedition.

Morgan went to Jamaica, and after dutifully giving a share of the spoils to the governor, left his former way of life and in a few years became governor himself. Strange to say, he then did more to suppress piracy than any of his predecessors. Calling in British warships, he thoroughly discredited buccaneering along the Spanish Main.

Through the influence of the Viceroy of Peru, steps were at once taken to rebuild Panama city. On October 31, 1672, the queen of Spain signed a decree changing the location of the city to its present site. The building of the new city was started on January 21, 1673. The new site was chosen for various reasons, chief of which was that it afforded better facilities for defense. The value of Ancon Hill for fortifications was mentioned frequently in the dispatches of the time. Money to carry on the work was to come largely from Peru, and those in charge were warned by the Spanish monarch to use care and judgment in its expenditure. The new city grew apace. Elaborate walls rose for its protection oceanward, and there was great laying out of streets and building of homes. These walls, which are among the most interesting sights of Panama to-day, cost a vast amount of money.

With Morgan's great raid, buccaneering as a business began to wane in the Spanish-American waters, but the Spanish ports of the Isthmus were not entirely neglected by the pirates. In 1679, Dampier, Sharp, Hawkins and other leaders of the later pirates raided Porto Bello, which had recovered some of its former glory. The town made little effort to defend itself, but it was sacked hurriedly — warrants were out for the pirates which, if served, would have meant hanging. They stopped at Bocas del Toro and again at the San Blas Islands. In this party, which later went to the Pacific to sack Santa Maria in the Gulf of San Miguel, were Dampier,

RUINS OF A SENTRY BOX

TOWER OF ST. ANASTASIUS

Ringrose and Lionel Wafer, who later became historians of the exploits. The last mentioned carried back to England a report that in one part of the Isthmus of Panama there were no mountains, a report which interested those who had long cast eyes of hope toward connecting the two oceans by water. Wafer's mistaken idea led to some interesting history in connection with canal projecting which will be mentioned later.

After varying fortunes this band of pirates, some three hundred and fifty strong, set out to attack the new city of Panama. Catching up with a Spanish boat in the Pacific, they were careless enough to allow it to get away and to carry intelligence of their coming. On April 23, 1680, the pirates arrived in the Bay of Panama, where a great naval battle was fought and won by them. The five Spanish men-of-war were not properly manned and proved unable to withstand the attack.

Though victorious in the naval engagement, the pirates did not attempt to land at Panama, contenting themselves instead with lying out in the bay and selling to the merchants goods which they had captured as spoils of the battle. A part of the time they spent at Taboga, consuming in all ten days in the waters of Panama Bay. Finally, after threatening to return later to sack the city, the pirates left for a cruise along the coast of South America.

After months of varying success the party split in two, those who did not care to follow Sharp, the commander of the expedition, sailing for the Gulf of San Miguel on the Pacific coast of the Isthmus. Dampier and Wafer were in this party of forty-four men who later undertook the perilous trip across the Isthmus to the Atlantic. The account of their hardships reads much like the story of Morgan's famous march. They were surrounded by hostile Indians, compelled to choose the most circuitous route to avoid contact with the Spaniards, forced to ford swollen streams and to flounder through almost impassable tropical jungle. Wafer, the surgeon of the party, met with an accident while drying out his powder one day, and with two companions was left behind to the mercy of the Indians. Good fortune was with him, however, for a few weeks later he and his comrades reached the Atlantic and found Dampier's sloop.

CHAPTER VII

THE LAND OF DREAMS

ANY detailed history of the Isthmus during the eighteenth century would be uninteresting, save perhaps the mention of an occasional conflict between the Spanish settlers and the Indians of Darien. In the accounts of piratical raids in the latter half of the seventeenth century, the Indian was an ever-present factor even in that part of the Isthmus that is now being so rapidly modernized by American enterprise. During the days of its glory Nombre de Dios was never free from danger of an attack by the Maroons or Cimmaroons, while Porto Bello, in later years, considered these tribes a not infrequent menace.

During the years from 1700 until far into the latter half of the century the savages of Darien not only resisted all attempts at settling their country, but made occasional forays into territory settled by the Spaniards. Attempts on the part of the Jesuit missionaries to penetrate the lower Isthmus met with repeated failure — often resulting in the pillage of their outposts and the massacre of the occupants.

Even to this day Yaviza, a town on one of the tributaries of the Tuyra River, founded by these Jesuit priests in 1740, is an outpost of the Darien Indians and remains largely forbidden ground. Beyond Yaviza the white man, unless he is a trader well known to the tribes, seldom ventures. The Indians of San Blas, frequent visitors to Colon, are the only type familiar to the resident of the Canal Zone.

But if desultory conflicts between the savage and the Spanish settler form the most exciting events of Isthmian history during the eighteenth century, they do not mean that Panama occupied no place in the minds of men across the sea. The world-famous Isthmus, with its vast possibilities, has been a place to dream about from the day of its discovery. Only a narrow strip of land in the inevitable path of the world's commerce!

Even before the dawn of the century of which we speak, one prominent man had dreamed of the commercial possibilities of the Isthmus. It was William Patterson, founder of the Bank of England, who seized upon the favorable report of Lionel Wafer, of piratical fame, to make the Isthmus the objective point of one of the most colossal schemes in history. That it failed miserably does not cast discredit upon the man who dreamed of its possibilities. Like the famous Mississippi Bubble, this Isthmian Bubble burst because it was ahead of its time.

SAN BLAS INDIANS AT ARMILLA

Patterson planned to establish on the Isthmus colonies that would control the key to the world's trade, and thus make great his own country, Scotland. With the idea of first controlling the trade between the Eastern and the Western hemispheres, he went among the merchants of Scotland to solicit funds. He raised £900,000, mostly among his own people, and in 1698, with twelve hundred colonists recruited in Scotland, sailed for the Isthmian seaboard.

Landing along the Isthmus of Darien not far from the spot made famous by Balboa and Pedrarias, the Scotch colonists named the small bay which they entered, New Caledonia. The place is known to-day as Puerto Escoces. Founding the towns of New Edinburg and St. Andrews, they had scarcely settled when the fevers of this infested coast devastated the colony, the settlers from bonny Scotland succumbing by hundreds. When Starvation stalked alongside the specter, Disease, the disheartened remnant returned to Scotland in June, 1699.

Not daunted, the company sent forth another party of colonists, thirteen hundred in number, the same year. It also returned, as did a third colony sent out in February, 1700. The last settlers might have remained had not the hostility of the Spaniards driven them away. Thus ended, at the sacrifice of an immense sum of money and of many lives, one man's scheme for converting Panama into commercial capital. In 1715, the Parliament of Great Britain, making tardy amends for a great man's misfortune, gave Patterson an indemnity of £18,241 for his losses in the Darien project.

A hundred years later another great man was dreaming of Panama in an altogether different fashion. Baron von Humboldt, German naturalist and traveler, during his well-known and fruitful voyage to Spanish America, found time to dream of the canal which he saw would some day connect the two oceans. He mentioned nine possible routes, some of them most visionary in the light of present-day knowledge, but he did not fail to include all the feasible ones. He computed the various elevations, and because of its advantages in this respect, named Panama as the most favorable route.

Another man whom we can imagine as dreaming of the commercial future of the American Isthmus before Humboldt visited it, was Lord Horatio Nelson, the great English Admiral. Long before the event at Trafalgar had given him undying fame, the English government had sent him in charge of an expedition to seize the lakes of Nicaragua with the idea of using them later in a scheme for controlling the interoceanic commerce. This was in 1780, when England and Spain were quarreling for possession of the Nicaraguan seaboard. Though Nelson planned to seize the whole strip of country from ocean to ocean, his expedition really accomplished little. Its commander injured his health in the attempt, and returned to England after barely dipping into the project.

In glancing over the names of individuals prominent in modern European history who found time to think about this great prospect across the seas, it is interesting to speculate what might have been the result had Louis Napoleon been successful in launching on the American Isthmus a scheme similar to that by which he sought to establish his power in Mexico. Even vaster designs may have actuated the ambitious emperor in his attempts to gain control of the Isthmus of Panama.

Louis was a prisoner of state under Louis Philippe when he first became interested in the Isthmus and especially in Nicaragua. Upon his escape from prison in 1846 he went to England and published articles on his views, comparing the future of the Isthmus to the past of Constantinople, whose geographical position rendered her the "Queen of the ancient world." But intrigues in France kept him too busy to push his scheme. He clung to it, however, and carried it to the point of having a canal route surveyed and of securing a concession from the Nicaraguan government. Though he never accomplished more than this because of his precarious position at home, it is worth while to remember that he saw into the possibilities of the Isthmus. Had Napoleon III been firmly seated on his throne, there is no telling what effect his intriguing might have had on the history of the Isthmus. He was, perhaps, still dreaming of it in 1870, when Germany descended upon France and put an end to his empire and to his career.

Then, too, Panama is a land of schoolboy dreams. No part of American history is more absorbing to the schoolboy than that which deals with exploration and discovery. What golden fancies have been woven about that old Spaniard who went to Florida to hunt for the "fountain of everlasting youth," or of him who marched on a conquering expedition up the Mississippi Valley and made the Indians believe he was a child of the Sun whom they dared not molest? We should not be fair to our younger readers if we failed to tell them that these same heroes, Ponce de Leon, De Soto and others equally well known, have had their place in the history of discovery at Panama. We but mention some of the best known of them.

Amerigo Vespucci, whose name was inadvertently given to the western hemisphere, cruised along the Gulf of Darien as early as 1499, and for the next eight years traveled up and down the mainland, many times touching the shores of Panama, in search of that strait which was believed to exist thereabouts. De Cosa and Pinzon, commanders respectively of the *Santa Maria* and the *Niña* on Columbus's first voyage, made early trips along the Isthmian coast in quest of the strait and of gold. De Soto, who goes down in fame as the discoverer of the Mississippi and is infamous because of his Indian-killing expedition along that same stream, explored the coast as far up as Yucatan. Cortez, the conqueror of Mexico, was one of the fathers of the plan to dig some kind of a waterway across the American Isthmus. Pizarro, the despoiler of Aztec civilization in Peru, played an important rôle in affairs of the Isthmus during those strenuous days following Balboa's startling discovery of the Pacific, a rôle which is a part of the Balboa story, already told.

Many more names might be mentioned; the most important must suffice, however, for it is time to tell what manner of place the Isthmus of Panama was, to attract so many Spanish explorers and adventurers. The land was a tropical jungle, differing very little from its present appearance. The flora and fauna which the Spanish pioneers saw were the same which greet the eye of the American hunter to-day when, armed with his Winchester, he sets out from a Canal Zone village to kill a deer, a jaguar or a mountain cow.

But how different the inhabitants! Instead of a

sparsely settled interior and a few towns, with a population all told of less than a half million in the whole Republic, the Isthmus of Panama then had two million people. From the agricultural plains of Chiriqui in the northernmost part to the mountain fastnesses of San Blas in the south, the Spaniards found Indians who were contented and prosperous. They were the Chibchas, who had reached a plane of civilization not unlike that of the Incas of Peru and the Aztecs of Mexico. In Chiriqui and neighboring northern provinces their culture was highest, due perhaps, not only to the influences of Aztec refinement, but to the richness of Mayan civilization in Yucatan, some of which had filtered down to the Isthmus.

The glories of this civilization are being unearthed in the province of Chiriqui every day. Within the past few years, a systematic study of this Indian culture has been made by digging up the buried evidences of it from the graves of the early race. Barrel after barrel of pottery has been shipped out of the province by scientists, curio-seekers and museums. A classification of these buried mementoes of a past age places the Isthmian Indian of the fifteenth century on a plane not far below his neighbors of Mexico and Peru.

These Indians had passed the stone and the bronze age. In many ways they gave evidence of

NATIVES POUNDING RICE

WASH DAY AT TABOGA

an Asiatic origin, as do other early American tribes. This is shown in their worship of the sun, stars and moon, and their use of the decimal system. Like the Asiatics, they had a calendar with a week of three days and a cycle of fifteen years. They were not cannibals, but offered human sacrifice as did the Aztecs. The Isthmian Indian was not warlike, nor did he have a strong centralized government such as the Incas enjoyed. These two causes account for his allowing the Spaniards to enslave him, make him a beast of burden and depopulate his race with amazing cruelties. The atrocious treatment to which he submitted practically exterminated the Isthmian Indian in a brief hundred years. That part of the original two million who were not wiped out, root and branch, became subdued, eventually intermarried with the conquering races and to-day their descendants reside in their native land as the modern Panamanians who are usually a mixture of Spanish and Indian.

One striking exception to this mixture of races is the San Blas Indian. Living in the almost inaccessible tropical mountains of southern Panama, this race, or collection of tribes, has kept the Indian blood pure. In appearance the San Blas Indian is typical. He has high cheek bones, copper color, large head, straight black hair, bow legs and low but powerful physique. The San Blas natives still enjoy the tribal life under a *cacique*, or chieftain. Though the men with their odd appearance and unique dress are a common and interesting sight on the streets of Colon, where they come to trade, the women never appear in public.

It is a San Blas tradition that no white man has ever been allowed to stay overnight in their country. So well intrenched is this tradition that the white visitor in the land is first invited, and then ordered, to leave San Blas before nightfall. The chief characteristic of these native Indians, who have so ably preserved their racial individuality, is their marked ability as sailors. A San Blas Indian can navigate a *cayuca* (a dugout with one sail) on almost any kind of sea. When the ocean liners have difficulty in making Limon Bay, the San Blas Indian sails skillfully into Colon harbor, after a run of perhaps fifty miles from his home down the coast. He brings a load of coconuts, hides, tropical fruits and a little gold. Though the yellow metal is known to exist in the San Blas country, the natives have never brought it in sufficient quantities to encourage white men to brave the native prejudices in attempting to exploit it.

(241)
SAN BLAS INDIAN WOMAN

An unusual snapshot secured by the authors

CHAPTER VIII

THE PANAMA OF TO-DAY

PANAMA has bulked so large in the imagination of men that it is worth while to take a short range view of the country and of its people as they are to-day. The Republic of Panama lies wholly in the tropics between 76° and 84° longitude and 7° and 10° latitude. The country is roughly rolling, rising in the extreme east to an elevation of about three thousand feet and in the west to nearly eleven thousand feet; the highest elevation being Chiriqui Volcano in the Province of Chiriqui. The average width of Panama is nearly one hundred miles and its length about four hundred miles.

The proximity of the oceans renders the climate moderate and equable. The temperature presents little variation; so little that American residents in the Canal Zone do not have recourse to the weather as a safe topic for desultory conversation. Variation in temperature averages from 70° at night to 92° in the daytime, and this average does not vary with the seasons. A wet season and a dry season take the place of spring, summer, fall and winter in the

States, the rainy period lasting eight months of the year. In May and June the precipitation is about what may be expected in the Central States; from July to January the rain is very excessive; while there is practically no rain in January, February, March and April.

The principal resources of Panama are its lumber and its agricultural possibilities. Little has been done in the development of either, but beginnings are now being made. In many parts of the Republic lumbering industries are springing up. English and American syndicates are financing them, and as fast as the mahogany, cocobolo, lignum-vitæ and other fine timber lands are cleared they are being converted into plantations, chiefly rubber and coconut.

The natives attach little value to the fine specimens of mahogany and other woods. They frequently hew a *cayuca* — a dugout boat — from a splendid mahogany log eighteen or twenty feet in length. Such a log in the United States, it is said, would be worth between two and three thousand dollars. Across a small stream near Chepo in the Bayana River country is a mahogany wood log forty feet long and five feet in diameter. In a piano factory in the States this log would be valued at several thousand dollars.

Within the borders of Panama there are more

than three hundred and fifty thousand people. Most of them live in small towns and villages. Panama and Colon are the largest cities, having respectively about thirty-five thousand and twenty thousand people. David and Boquete are considerable communities in the west. With these exceptions the towns in Panama are small groups of bamboo huts, thatched to keep out sun and rain.

In the jungle one frequently comes upon a thatched hut where dwell the farmer and his wife with a family of seven or eight children. The furnishings of these primitive homes are rude; gourds and coconut shells are the chief culinary utensils. The bare ground is more often than not the bed, the table, the chair, the workbench and very possibly the chicken roost. An old-fashioned muzzle-loading rifle and a powder horn combine utility and adornment. When a stranger appears the whole family gather about to welcome him and to minister to his needs as well as they can with their limited facilities.

A few coconut trees, a small patch of bananas and a garden, medium sized and well grown with weeds, are usually the only evidences of any provision for the future. But the future does not trouble these humble creatures; they rely on Nature and *mañana* to supply their simple needs. Suffrage, tariff and kindred interests do not touch them. There is no necessity for providing against winter, to incite them to activity; there is little to stimulate the ambition or to sharpen the wits. These residents of Panama's interior have very little need for communication with the outside world, since the daily routine consists in getting a living from Nature as she presents opportunity for it at their very doors. Yet the native in the "bush" visits his neighbors, makes an occasional trip to the nearest village, and is beginning to take more than a desultory interest in the politics of his country. He was an important factor in the election of the president of Panama in 1912, and the Liberal Party, representing progress and advancement, receives his support.

Occasionally one finds evidences that the native of the interior is beginning to know the outside world. A soap box bearing the brand of a well-known American firm may serve as his washstand. Cheap lithographs sometimes adorn the walls of his cottage. The farmer himself wears a pair of cottonade trousers and a hickory shirt, both products of foreign manufacture; while the members of his family disport themselves in calico and gingham.

The people of the interior are devout Catholics — as are all Latin American people. In every interior community the church fêtes and festivals are observed with punctilious regard. Indeed, the most vivid impressions of this religious feeling can be obtained in the rural sections. At Taboga there is an

I. CHIRIQUI VOLCANO AND THE BOQUETE VALLEY
II. A NATIVE HOTEL, DAVID

I. PATIO SCENE NEAR DAVID
II. PRESIDENTIAL ELECTION DAY, DAVID

impressive celebration every Easter. Holy Week, which precedes Easter Sunday, is devoted to the observances of this ceremony; and from Friday until Sunday there is a graphic portrayal of the events of Christ's passion which those days commemorate. Former residents of the village return for this passion play, lodgings are scarce and the village is filled with visitors. All the members of the local parish participate in this devotional ceremony. The young men, dressed as Roman soldiers, guard the sanctuary in the church. The maidens of the village have their share in the ceremony in honor of the Virgin Mary, and all the villagers find place in the nightly processions in which the sanctuary and the images from the church are carried through the village, on floats. All these ceremonies are characterized by a reverent devotion. One feels that during them Christianity is, to these simple people, a living, pulsating faith.

In contrast with the type of native found in the interior sections, there are the purely Spanish people who are energetic and progressive. Many of them have homes that would be a credit to an American farmer. Their farms are well kept and show thrift not inferior to that found in our best American communities. A few such farms are to be seen in the neighborhood of Panama City and in the western provinces, where conditions are more favorable for agriculture. This is particularly true around David and Boquete.

The better class of Spanish residents in Panama City and Colon are refined, cultivated and intelligent people, among whom the canal builders have found intimate and interesting friends. These people have been educated in American and in foreign universities. The Panamanians of the first families are regular attendants at the semimonthly balls given by Commission employees at the Tivoli Hotel. Once an entry is gained to their charming homes the visitor begins a delightful friendship.

At present the one absorbing interest in Panama is the construction of the great canal. Contrary to the popular notion, the Canal takes a southeasterly direction from the Atlantic Ocean to the Pacific Ocean. The Canal Zone, a strip of land extending five miles on each side of the canal, cuts the Republic of Panama into two almost equal parts. Except that the jungle has been cleared away near the scene of operations, the country covered by our jurisdiction is not in any essential particular different from the adjacent country. The present scheme of government for the Canal Zone, after the completion of the canal, provides for the return of the Zone to its original jungle growth, as it prohibits any settlement there and any agricultural development. Such a tropical jungle would be an invaluable aid in the protection of the canal against possible invasion by land.

The population of the Canal Zone differs materially from that of the Republic of Panama. In the Canal Zone one finds a most cosmopolitan people, gathered together from the four corners of the earth to help build the great waterway. In addition to the Americans, there are in the employ of the Isthmian Canal Commission West Indians, East Indians, Spaniards, Colombians, Panamanians, American Negroes, Italians, Greeks and what not. Of course the most important members of this complex working force are the Americans.

Americans in the Canal Zone are not so far out of the world as one might think. Indeed, to them the Canal Zone has become an American community, with its churches, clubs, entertainment halls and typical American homes. The Commission employee who has come from the United States has brought his institutions with him. After a strenuous week's work he finds the same recreation on Sunday that engages thousands of his countrymen at home. He has his library table with its books, magazines and newspapers. He may go to church, and will surely send his children to Sunday School. He enjoys a Sunday dinner not unlike that which you would have at home. Then in the afternoon he may go swimming or to a baseball game. In the evening he may attend a sacred concert at the Y.M.C.A. Club House. Or perhaps he has spent the day in Panama City, where he watched the lottery drawing at ten o'clock on Sunday morning, drove into the savannas in the afternoon and took dinner at the Central or the Tivoli, while listening to a concert by the I.C.C. band or the National band of the Republic.

If it was the Sunday on which the I.C.C. band gives its concert in his home town he certainly stayed at home; for the excellent concerts of this organization are important events in the social life of each Canal Zone village. The Commission band is composed of employees who have weekly rehearsals and weekly concerts under the direction of a trained leader. The band is supported from Commission funds, each member receiving a compensation for his services. The music director is employed in that capacity and devotes his entire time to musical affairs given under official direction.

Social life among the Americans in the Zone finds its outlet in dances, dinner parties, bridge parties, moving picture shows, beach parties, picnics, tennis, bowling, bathing, and boating. The men talk politics with as much fervor as if they were voting in the various political contests at home. During the national campaign numerous straw elections, preceded by speech making, political rallies and campaigning for favorite candidates, add a realistic

I. THE PANAMA LOTTERY
II. SKATING ON SEA WALL

I. PEARL ISLANDS, PANAMA BAY
II. PEARL DIVERS

AT FORT LORENZO
A popular picnic resort for the Canal builders

feature to this form of play which really keeps the employee interested in his citizenship.

The craving for entertainment which every normal American carries with him is gratified in the Canal Zone by the managers of the Y.M.C.A. Club House. They bring entertainers from the States; and get up local talent minstrel shows, comic operas, vaudeville shows and concerts. During the winter months grand opera companies sing *Carmen, Il Trovatore* and other classics, in Spanish, at the National Theatre in Panama City. Americans form an enthusiastic and appreciative part of the audience at these operas. Each year at least one circus comes to the Canal Zone on its way to South America; everybody goes.

Perhaps nowhere in the world is July Fourth celebrated with more enthusiasm than in Panama. Each employee contributes toward a fund for this celebration, which includes patriotic exercises, athletic contests, aquatic events and baseball games, throughout the day; and an elaborate display of fireworks at night. Thousands of dollars are spent on these fireworks, and valuable prizes are given the winners in the athletic and aquatic contests.

The non-American members of the Canal Zone population are very interesting. In the foreign sections of the towns John Chinaman, who "likee Milika man vellee much," distributes his oriental goods. John is not a one-price merchant, and he seldom lets a seriously inclined customer escape without relieving him of some of his substance. John's children attend the American schools, and none stand higher than they. It may be said of John that while he is an enterprising citizen his enterprise never gets him entangled in the law. His crookedness is not unlike that of some of our noted American captains of industry — it is usually legitimate so far as courts and the law are concerned.

The East Indian also has his shops in the native sections; linens, laces and silks are his principal stock in trade. Following the custom of his race, he does not rely wholly on his shop; he goes out after business, and he may be seen any day and in any community with a great pack swung over his back, visiting the American housewife on the Isthmus. A day or two after pay day his tribe are especially active. Like the Chinaman, he adjusts the price of a commodity to the experience and the financial strength of his customer. The sign boards of these venders make interesting reading. Sing On, for instance, sells "disturbances of many varieties to the thirsty."

A census taken in March, 1912, presents some interesting figures regarding the population of the Canal Zone. Great Britain furnishes (largely from its West Indian domain) the greatest number of inhabitants, 30,859; the United States comes next, with 11,850; Panama supplies 7636; Spain 4305; France, 2760; Colombia, 1521; Greece, 1291. Other countries are represented by various numbers of people; from Italy, with 812, down to Roumania, Liberia and Bulgaria, which have one each. The grand total is 62,810, of which 45,163 are males and 17,647 females. These figures do not include the employees of the United States government in Panama and in Colon. Classified by races, the population of the Canal Zone is as follows: White, 20,063; Black, 38,425; Indian, 648; Yellow, 527; Hindu, 381; Filipino, 2; mixed, 11,636. Of the 11,850 American citizens enumerated, 1375 are from Pennsylvania, 1372 from New York, 692 from Ohio, 453 from Illinois, 386 from Massachusetts, 382 from Indiana.

It is estimated that at the time of the last census there were 42,000 people in the employ of the Canal Commission. Practically all the white Americans are employed in supervisory positions or in positions requiring skill, while the unskilled labor is done by day laborers, most of whom are West Indians and Spaniards or Spanish-speaking people.

CHAPTER IX

THE PANAMA RAILROAD

SIMON BOLIVAR, the South American patriot, had visions of the importance of an Isthmian canal in his scheme of a unified Latin America. In 1829 he employed two engineers, Lloyd, an Englishman, and Falcmar, a Swede, to survey a route across the Isthmus. This survey resulted in nothing as far as Bolivar's plans were concerned, but it later became the route of the Panama Railroad, the first transcontinental railway in the western hemisphere and one of the important engineering accomplishments of the nineteenth century.

In 1846, the United States made a treaty with New Granada, now Colombia, which was destined to have a far-reaching effect on all future schemes for connecting the Atlantic and the Pacific. It gave the United States the exclusive right of transit across the Isthmus from the Chiriqui Lagoon to the Atrato River. This included all routes — road, railway or canal. The treaty came just at the time we were acquiring Oregon and were going into a war of territorial acquisition with Mexico. With the securing of new territory on the Pacific came an imperative need for some line of communication across the Isthmus. So under the new treaty, John L. Stephens, a New York writer, traveler and prominent man of affairs, went to Bogota in 1850 to secure a franchise for a railroad which was to be financed and built by American capital.

He completed his negotiations that year, a company was organized, and there began a terrific battle with tropical nature which was to end triumphantly five years later in a completed railway across the Isthmus. The promoters of the railroad were John L. Stephens, W. H. Aspinwall and Henry Chauncey. To commemorate the names of these capitalists there is a rather mediocre statue on Colon Beach.

The company started work in May, 1850, with Colonel G. M. Totten as chief engineer. From what we know of conditions at the time, it must have been a beginning to dishearten any but those of most profound faith and of determined mind. We may imagine a rowboat scraping the coral at Manzanillo Island, a few white men and natives leaping from the boat, then the cutting of a path through the almost impenetrable jungle. Manzanillo Island, now the site of Colon and Cristobal, was then a low coral island — a malaria infested swamp.

Porto Bello, twenty miles away, with its excellent

harbor, would have made a much better Atlantic terminus for the railroad. It was, in fact, the logical terminus from its historic rôle as the Atlantic end of the old Royal Road. Mr. Tracy Robinson, in his excellent book of personal reminiscences, gives as the reason why Porto Bello was not chosen the inability of the railroad company to secure a right of way there at a reasonable price. A New Yorker owned the available land at Porto Bello, and he held out for a price which the young company felt that it could not pay. As a consequence, the excellent harbor was given up. Manzanillo Island in Limon or Navy Bay was the next best location.

So antagonistic to human invasion was this coral island and the jungle back of it, that work was extremely slow. By October 1, 1851, a year and a half after the start, the steel rails had been laid as far as Gatun, six miles from Colon. Could the railroad have been completed at this time — an impossible task — a fortune would have been earned by it from the Forty-niners and the stream of gold seekers who, in the few years following, chose the Panama route as the best way of getting to California. A steel girded roadbed from the Atlantic to the Pacific would have furnished a more convenient and less perilous route than that from the Chagres to Cruces or Gorgona, and thence by mule to Panama.

As it was, the railroad did a profitable business

before its completion, transporting immigrants and fortune hunters westward bound. It is said that the road earned $2,000,000 during the time of its construction.

By 1852 the most difficult part of the work had been done, as the road had been carried through the swamps between Colon and Gatun and the famous Black Swamp between Lion Hill and Ahorca Lagarta which were the great obstacles in the construction. When the road was half completed, work stopped for almost a year, but it was taken up again, and the battle against disease, difficulties and tropical dangers was carried to successful completion on January 27, 1855. On that day the last spike was driven at Culebra. At a cost of $7,000,000 — $140,000 a mile — and the loss of enough lives to give rise to the story that every tie of the railroad represented a human life — the big task was finished.

With the completion of the railroad the malaria infested swamp on the coral island at the Atlantic terminus was transformed into a small city, which gradually grew into a seaport of consequence. The town of Colon, born with the railroad sixty years ago, is now a flourishing little city with prospects brighter than ever before in its turbulent career. With the canal an accomplished fact it may in time outstrip even Panama in commercial importance. Colon is still mediæval in makeup, but American enterprise is being injected every day into its commercial life. A $300,000 fire on March 23, 1911, which wiped out a fourth of the poorly built part of the town, will some day be looked back upon as a boon to the place.

Originally, in 1852, the town was called Aspinwall in honor of one of the promoters of the railroad. The place would still be called by that name but for the objection of the government of Colombia, which insisted that the name be changed to Colon. Americans refused to recognize it as Colon until the South American Republic stopped delivering mail addressed to Aspinwall. The dispute at one time assumed almost the dignity of a diplomatic incident, Colombia refusing to issue an *exequatur* to an American consul at "Aspinwall." Since it was a town within the jurisdiction of Colombia, there was nothing the American government could do but acquiesce.

Colon has a number of interesting buildings whose associations date back to the early days of the railroad. The weather-beaten Washington Hotel on Colon Beach recently replaced by the "New Washington" breasted the trade winds for a half century. Corpus Christi Church has pointed its spires skyward since 1865. The old station, four blocks north of the present modern structure, was the terminus of the railroad for many years and was not turned into a freight station until the present *régime*.

The story of the securing of the railroad's franchise is interesting. The terms of this franchise, granted to Stephens by the Republic of Colombia, were later the cause of much worry to the railroad. Under it the road could be bought by the government of Colombia in twenty years for $5,000,000, and at the end of forty-nine years it reverted to that Republic without payment. In 1867 a new franchise was secured. The life of the franchise was extended ninety-nine years, but this concession entailed the cash payment to Colombia of $1,000,000 and a yearly bonus of $250,000.

From the start, high rates were charged by the Panama Railroad. Twenty-five dollars for a first class passage across the Isthmus, ten dollars for second class and five cents per pound for baggage seems rather high to tourists from the two cents a mile states in the Union who object to the fare of two dollars and forty cents now charged. They feel better when told what the fare used to be. It is said that in the old days the passenger who objected to the high tariff gained nothing by attempting to walk across the Isthmus. The railroad owned the only passable route and charged travelers the full fare whether they went afoot or in a railway coach.

For the first ten years of its career the railroad did an enormous business. Shares of the stock shot up to one hundred above par and stayed there for a part of the time. A statement published when the railroad was fifty years old shows that almost forty million dollars in dividends had been earned up to that time. In 1869 the Overland Route was completed in the United States and much of the transcontinental business left the Panama Railroad. About this time, too, the railroad, laboring under the mistaken idea that it could dictate terms to the shippers via the Isthmus, lost a vast amount of business through the establishment of steamship lines by rival companies.

When the French company began operations, as related in Chapter II, it bought sixty-eight seventieths of the railroad stock for $18,000,000. But when the United States bought the road from the French, instead of paying the $18,000,000 the French had given for it, our government included the purchase price of the railroad in the $40,000,000 we paid the New Panama Canal Company.

In addition to all rights, franchises, properties and unfinished work on the canal which the French had left, we acquired from the company all the capital stock of the Panama Railroad which it held. By the provisions of the Spooner Bill this was to be not less than 68,863 shares out of a total of 70,000 shares. In figuring the amount of money which the United States should pay the French company for

IN THE JUNGLE

I. GATHERING COCONUTS
II. A PINEAPPLE PLANTATION

all its properties in Panama, the value of the railroad was estimated at $7,000,000, the original capitalization of the road. In January, 1905, the United States, on the recommendation of Secretary Taft, bought the remainder of the outstanding stock, which was less than two seventieths of the whole. For this stock the United States government paid $275 per share, or $312,675. By this acquisition of outstanding stock held by private individuals, the United States became sole owner of the Panama Railroad and of its steamship lines from Colon to New York. As stated before, however, the road is operated as a private corporation by a board of directors.

CHAPTER X

DIPLOMACY OF TWO HUNDRED AND FIFTY YEARS

THE completion of an American canal under American control will mark the culmination not only of years of physical endeavor, but also of centuries of statecraft. Contemporary with the dreams of Isthmian canal projectors was the activity of the diplomats of many nations. The countries chiefly interested in securing this strip of land were England, Spain, France, Colombia and the United States.

Next to Spain, whose interest dates from the days of Columbus, England has been a factor in Isthmian affairs longer than any other nation. As early as 1650 British freebooters were settling in desultory fashion in Honduras and Nicaragua. Spain protested, but twenty years later a treaty between the two countries confirmed the English in their possessions, though Spain two years afterward insisted that this treaty applied only to Jamaica and to the other islands England was occupying. England, however, maintained that the treaty referred to the mainland as well, and began a series of maneuvers in which, diplomatically, she far excelled her rivals.

During this same century British adventurers, negroes from a Dutch slaver and the native Indians formed a hybrid colony along that part of the Nicaraguan shore known as the Mosquito coast. This settlement in the land of the Mosquito Indian became an entering wedge for England, who landed troops and occupied the place in 1740. In 1775 the British colony in Mosquito Land was made into a dependency of Jamaica. Protests of Spain resulted in little, for while England treated with her each time, the Spaniards were outwitted by superior diplomacy.

In 1779 England gave up her claim to the land, keeping, however, a strip at Belize (now British Honduras) in which to "cut trees." A few years later Spain was induced to enlarge this tree cutting area. By 1825 England had established a regency at Bluefields, and ten years later the land of the Mosquitoes was organized as a province under the name of British Honduras. Finally, in 1860, by a diplomatic *coup* in which she induced Nicaragua to acknowledge the validity of English claims to Honduras, Great Britain became an established fixture along that part of the Isthmus.

Since England had so firm a hold on Nicaragua she naturally became the chief nation with which the American government had to deal when at last it became interested in the Isthmus. The United

States had been slow to appreciate the great opportunity almost at her door. In 1835 some interest was manifested in the Isthmus, when on the motion of Senator Henry Clay, President Jackson sent Charles Biddle there to investigate the possibility of a canal. This mission had no definite results, but finally the United States, aroused by the need of communication with her new possessions in the northwest and the far west, negotiated a treaty with New Granada which was ratified by the United States Senate on June 10, 1846.

By this treaty the United States secured the sole right of transit across the Isthmus on any routes opened by road, railroad or canal from the Atrato River northward to the Chiriqui Lagoon. This embraced the Isthmus of Panama in its limited definition, and was the treaty which made possible the Panama Railroad whose franchise was secured four years later. Other terms of the treaty were that American citizens were to be put on the same basis as citizens of New Granada as to concessions, immunities, tolls, etc. In return for these concessions, the United States agreed to maintain the neutrality of any lines of transit which might be built and to guarantee the rights of New Granada against aliens. The American government also guaranteed the sovereignty of New Granada.

Flushed with the success of this treaty, the United

CITY OF PANAMA, FROM ANCON HILL

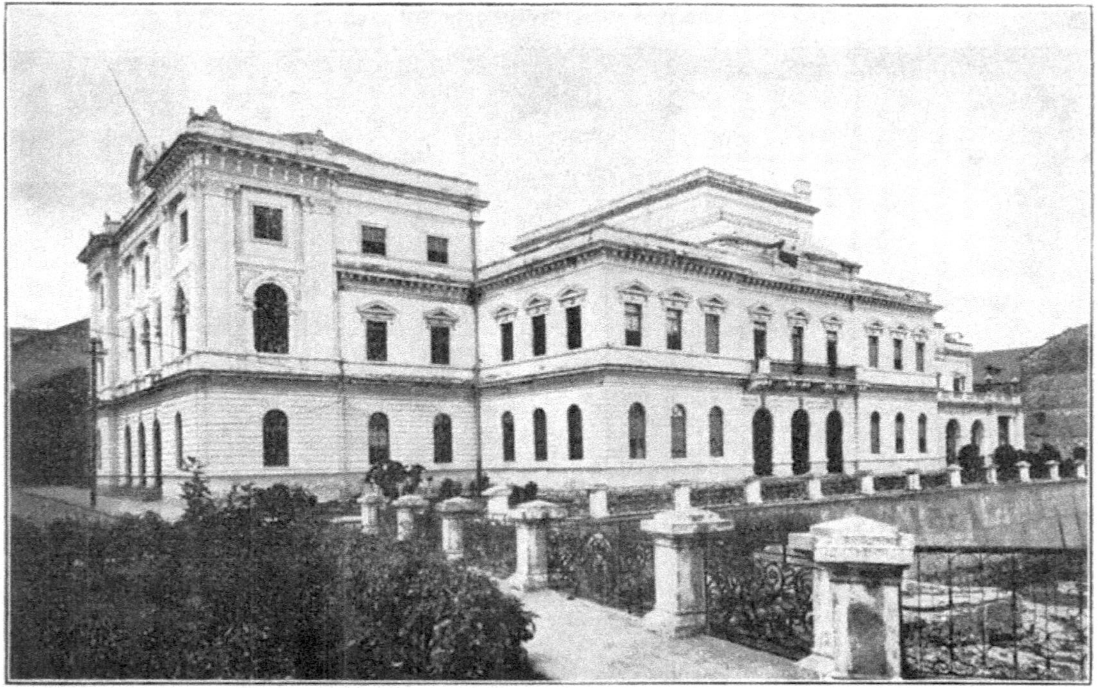

THE GOVERNMENT PALACE, PANAMA

States, three years later, sent Elijah Hise to Nicaragua, and he attempted to create there the conditions we had just established at the Lower Isthmus of Panama. But there were complications, due to the fact that England was interested in Nicaragua, whereas she had not been particularly interested in Panama. The government at Washington recalled Hise and sent down E. G. Squier, who had, however, views similar to those of his predecessor. He made a treaty with Nicaragua, guaranteeing to that Republic the sovereignty over the territory traversed by the proposed canal. But this was a direct slap at England, which was asserting sovereignty over the Atlantic terminus of such a route. England retaliated by taking steps to seize from Honduras Tiger Island in the Gulf of Fonseca, which would give her control of the Pacific terminus. Her ostensible ground for this was the failure of Honduras to pay an old debt.

In return, Mr. Squier hastily made a treaty with Nicaragua by which she ceded Tiger Island to the United States. This created a situation which would mean an open breach with England unless something was speedily done. Something was done which American statesmen had cause to regret for the next fifty years. This something was the Clayton-Bulwer treaty. Since the political situation in the United States at this time rendered war with England inexpedient, this treaty was accepted as the only alternative in sight.

By this treaty, which was proclaimed in 1850, the neutrality of an Isthmian canal was guaranteed to the extent that neither government was to build or to fortify it, nor ever to enter into an alliance with any Central American country to that end. Any company which cared to undertake the project was to be jointly protected by England and by the United States, and they were to invite other nations to join in this protection. There were to be two free ports, one at each end of the canal. This principle of neutrality was to be applied to all canal routes on the Isthmus.

Naturally England did not apply the treaty to British Honduras or to Mosquito Land, and so she successfully kept the United States out of the Isthmus while relinquishing nothing. The difficulty in which the United States had placed herself was not realized for some years. The events leading up to the Civil War and the war itself kept the American government busy with matters at home. Once her own house was again in order, however, the United States had an opportunity to appreciate the full significance of the treaty.

In 1866 Secretary Seward voiced a growing popular sentiment by suggesting that the United States buy Tiger Island and abrogate the Clayton-Bulwer treaty. Under Presidents Buchanan and Lincoln the American government had begun to feel the need of a freer rein on the Isthmus. Lincoln at one time considered a plan to establish colonies of emancipated slaves near the Chiriqui Lagoon, along the Costa Rican shore line. President Grant advocated the bold policy of an "American Canal under American control," but the Senate in 1869 and 1870 refused to ratify treaties with Nicaragua looking toward an Isthmian waterway.

The undercurrent of sentiment against our limitations on the Isthmus came to the surface again when De Lesseps was said to be trying to influence Colombia to abrogate the treaty of 1846 and to permit him to build a canal under French control. The determined attitude of President Hayes caused De Lesseps to abandon his attempt and to organize a private company, which solicited funds in America as well as in France. President Hayes applied the Monroe Doctrine to the De Lesseps case.

For years the agitation for an American built canal controlled by America recurred with each new canal project, and always it ran against the Clayton-Bulwer treaty. When the United States was at war with Spain, an event occurred which thoroughly aroused the American people. Admiral Cervera's fleet was in Atlantic waters, and it was thought that the *Oregon*, one of the biggest battleships of the

United States, was needed to reënforce the American Atlantic squadron. The *Oregon* was at San Francisco and had to make the long and perilous trip around the Horn. In suspense the American public watched the daily progress of the ship on her long journey as reported through the newspapers. The fact that she made a superb voyage and was not needed after all, did not alter the firm conviction in American minds that a canal must be built for just such emergencies if for no other purpose.

In 1900, two years later, the United States was negotiating the Hay-Pauncefote treaty, which was to make possible the American canal.

The Hay-Pauncefote treaty, ratified December 16, 1901, makes the following provisions: First, abrogates the Clayton-Bulwer treaty. Second, gives the United States power to construct, operate and control a canal. Third, gives the United States a free hand over the canal in time of war. Fourth, forbids the blockading of the canal but does not forbid our fortifying it.

Thus ended the years of diplomacy leading up to the construction of the canal. That the United States was the logical builder of such a canal became as evident to England as to ourselves. After the French *fiasco*, this was the only solution of the problem.

The matter of fortification was definitely settled

I. CATHEDRAL PLAZA, PANAMA
II. INSTALLING THE WATER SYSTEM, PANAMA

DIPLOMACY OF TWO HUNDRED AND FIFTY YEARS 279

in the spring of 1911, when the House of Representatives of the United States voted an appropriation of $3,000,000 for that purpose. This action of the American Congress, and the steps since taken to stud the Isthmian ports with forts, settles forever the diplomatic question of whether or not we have actually acquired from England the right to fortify the canal. Even after the Hay-Pauncefote treaty was ratified and as late as the fall of 1910, there were people in the United States who insisted that the American government had bound itself not to fortify this great waterway. However, a careful investigation of the diplomatic provisions of the Anglo-American treaty convinced the Administration and the Congress of the United States, that, by omitting all reference to the question of fortification, the makers of the treaty meant to leave the government of the United States free to do just as it chose in the matter. Naturally, it chose to fortify the canal.

Such is Panama's story — a story of the search for the New Route to India. Columbus came this way in quest of a more direct route to the wealth of the Orient. Cortez believed in the practicability of securing an all-water route by the construction of an Isthmian canal. At various times and by various peoples surveys have been made, but in each case the project has ended where it began, and it was not till 1879, when the French launched upon the undertaking, that any real canal digging was done. To early Spanish enterprise the world owed the first transisthmian highway; to American enterprise its transisthmian railway, and to American enterprise it is indebted for the severing of the continents and the joining of the Atlantic ocean with the Pacific.

As we have shown, the idea of a transisthmian canal has been contemporaneous with the beginnings and growth of the romantic little country of Panama. And it is a noteworthy coincidence that the circumstance which gave birth to the Republic of Panama was the same which put the canal project in a way to materialize the NEW ROUTE TO INDIA.

INDEX

Ahorca Lagarta, 261.
Alhajuela, 55, 66, 70.
Amador, Dr., 22, 25.
America, Discovery of, 159.
Americans in Canal Zone, 37, 124, 134, 151.
Ancon (city), 90, 118, 137, 141.
Ancon, The, 109.
Ancon Hill, 222.
Antonelli (explorer), 3.
Aspinwall (town), 262.
Aspinwall, W. H., 259.
Atlantic Ocean, 1-2, 44.
Atrato River, 171, 258, 270.
Auditor of the Canal Zone, 135, 143.
Avila, Pedro Arias de, *see* Pedrarias.
Aztecs, 235-236.

Balboa, Vasco Nuñez de, 1, 93, 168-178, 180, 231, 235.
Balboa (city), 47, 90, 178.
Balboa Hill, 175.
Barbacoas, 217.
Bas Obispo, 77, 81, 100.
Bastidas, Roderigo de, 165-166, 168-169, 191.
Bastimentos, Isle of, 164.
Bayana River, 244.
Belize (British Honduras), 269.

Beri-beri in Canal Zone, 121.
Biddle, Charles, 270.
Bishop, Joseph Bucklin, 42.
Blackburn, Jo. C. S., 135.
Black Swamp, 66, 261.
Bluefields, 269.
Bocas del Toro, 222.
Bocas del Toro, Province of, 27.
Bogota, 18, 20, 25, 259.
Bohio, 65, 69, 70-71, 76.
Bolivar, Simon, 19, 258.
Boquete, 245, 250.
Breakwaters, 34, 47.
British Honduras, 269, 274.
Brodley, Captain, 211-215.
Brunet, Joseph, 14.
Buchanan, President James, 275.
Bunau-Varilla, Philippe, 25.

Caledonia, 172.
Caledonian Route, 175.
California, 260.
Campêche, 200.
Campêche Bay, 179.
Canal project, The :
    French Attempt, The, 7-14.
    Interest of other nations in, 2-13.
    Interest of the United States in, 4, 17-19, 268-280.

Canal project, The:
  Possible routes considered, 3–4, 17, 175.
  Possible types considered, 7, 10, 13, 41, 47.
  American Canal, The: construction of, 42–44, 48–94; cost of, 8, 14, 19, 29, 43, 47, 100, 107, 112, 132, 136; statistics regarding, 42–43, 47; water supply, 62–66, 70.
Canal Zone, The:
  Acquisition of, 14, 17, 97.
  Americans in, 110, 133–134, 251–256.
  Area and natural features of, 19, 28, 69–71, 77, 81–86, 107, 111–112, 149, 250–251.
  Jurisdiction in, 19, 28–29, 97–98, 111, 276–279.
  Occupation of, 134.
  Other nationalities in, 134, 251, 256–257.
  Politics in, 146, 252, 255.
  Schools in, 132–133, 135, 137, 145–149, 151.
  Statistics regarding, 43, 121, 256–257.
Canals, Comparison of, 47.
Canal Record, The, 99, 150, 154.
Cape Horn, 206, 276.
Caribbean Sea, 30, 44, 165.
Cartagena, 170, 180, 190, 211.
Castilla del Oro Country, 171.
Castle Chagre (Fort San Lorenzo), 211.
Castle Gloria, 191.

Cathay, 160, 163.
Central Avenue, Panama, 111.
Central Hotel, 252.
Cervera, Admiral Pascual, 275.
Chagres (city), 184.
Chagres (port), 188.
Chagres River, 10, 33, 41, 51–52, 57, 62, 65–66, 70, 76–78, 151, 164, 184, 188, 211, 215–216, 260.
Charles V, of Spain, 2, 3.
Chauncey, Henry, 259.
Chepo, 244.
Chibcha Indians, 236.
Chicago, 126.
Chief Engineer of the Isthmian Canal Commission, 43, 85, 89, 99, 155.
China, 160.
Chinese, 134, 137, 255–256.
Chiriqui, Province of, 27, 236, 243.
Chiriqui Lagoon, 163, 258, 270, 275.
Chiriqui Volcano, 243.
Cimmaroon Indians, 227.
Cipango, 160.
Civil War (in the United States), 4, 274.
Clay, Senator Henry, 270.
Clayton-Bulwer treaty, 273–276.
Cocle, Province of, 27.
Colombia, Republic of:
  Negotiations with France, 9, 17–19, 166.
  Negotiations with United States, 17–20, 258–259, 262–263.

Colombia, Republic of :
  Relations with Panama, 19–26, 268.
  Relations with Spain, 19.
Colon (city), 25–26, 28, 34, 111–112, 118, 134, 142, 166, 228, 245, 250.
Colon, Province of, 27.
Cólon Beach, Statue at, 259.
Colon Harbor, 44, 191, 240.
Columbus, Christopher, 1–2, 30, 33, 159–168, 178, 191, 235, 279.
Comogre (Indian chief), 171.
Compagnie Universelle du Canal Interoceanique, see Universal Interoceanic Company.
Concha (Colombian Minister), 19.
Confederación Granadina, 20.
Constantinople, 233.
Contractor's Hill, 82.
Cordillera Mountains, 33.
Corozal, 104.
Corpus Christi Church, 262.
Cortez, Hernando, 2, 3, 235, 279.
Costa Rica, 163, 275.
Coupon Books, 131, 154.
Courts of Justice in the Canal Zone, 133, 136, 142–144, 150–151.
Cristobal, 34, 71, 77, 104, 131, 137, 141, 167, 259.
Cristobal, The, 109.
Crocodiles, River of (Chagres River), 164.
Cruces, 184, 187, 190–191, 202, 217, 220, 260.

Cuba, 163, 207.
Cucaracha Slide, 85.
Culebra (town), 71, 78, 86, 104, 261.
Culebra Cut, 42, 48, 70, 72, 76–89.
Culebra Slide, 82, 85, 141.

Damage claims against I. C. C., 76, 151.
Dampier, William, 196, 222–226.
Darien (town), 227.
Darien, Gulf of, 164–165, 169–172, 234.
Darien, Isthmus of, 3, 231.
David, 245, 250.
Davis, Major General George W., 134.
Declaration of Independence of Panama, 21–22, 26.
De Cosa (explorer), 235.
De Leon, Ponce, 234.
De Lesseps, Count Ferdinand, 7–13, 167, 275.
De Lesseps Buildings, 34.
Denver, 61.
De Soto, Hernando, 234–235.
Devol, Colonel C. A., 101.
Dikes, 47.
Dominican friars, 3.
Drake, Sir Francis, 4, 196–207.
Dutch pirates, 206, 208.
Dutch settlers in Panama, 192.

East Indians, 134, 251.
Empire (city), 82, 104, 141, 149.

Employees of I. C. C., 34, 72, 110, 125, 138, 141, 146, 154, 251.
"Gold" employees, 101–104.
"Silver" employees, 101–102, 104.
Encisco, Martin Fernandez de, 169–171, 176.
England:
Explorations under, 196–204, 206–207.
Interest in Panama, 4, 134, 210, 231–232, 268–269, 273–276.
Relations with the United States, 269, 273–276.
Esquemeling (historian), 206, 208–209, 211, 216–217, 219.
Eugénie, Empress, of France, 166.
Exclusion laws against Chinese and Syrians, 137.

Ferdinand, King of Spain, 163.
Feuille, Judge Frank, 151.
Flamenco Island, 90.
Fluviograph stations, 55, 70–71.
Fonseca, Gulf of, 273.
Fortification of the Canal, 28, 153, 276, 279.
Fort Jeronimo, 191–192.
France:
Explorations under, 203–204, 207.
Frenchmen in Panama, 115, 199.
Interest in Canal project, 4, 233–234, 268; attempt to construct, 7–14, 38, 41–42, 76, 155, 199, 264, 276, 279.
Negotiations with Colombia, 9, 17–19; with the United States, 17–19, 264, 267.
Francisco River, 203.

Galvano (Spanish historian), 163.
Gamboa, 70.
Gatun (city), 37–41, 43–44, 66, 70, 76, 78, 100, 104, 141, 260–261.
Gatun Cocktail, 66.
Gatun Dam, 42, 48–52.
Gatun Lake, 30, 42, 57, 65, 76, 94, 100, 151.
Germans, 134, 232.
Germany, 234.
Goethals, Colonel George W., 43, 85, 89, 99, 155.
Gold Hill, 81–82, 86.
Gold-seeking Expeditions, 165, 171, 177, 200–204, 240, 260.
Gorgas, Dr. W. C., 114.
Gorgona, 76–77, 100, 104, 141, 175, 260.
Governor of the Canal Zone, 134.
Governor of Panama, 209–211, 215, 217.
Gracias á Dios (town), 163.
Gracias á Dios, Cape, 169.
Grant, President Ulysses S., 275.

Great Khan of China, 160.
Greeks, 134, 251.
Guinea town, 192, 195.

Haiti, 30, 163–165, 171, 196.
Havana, 114.
Hawkins (pirate), 222.
Hawkins, Sir John, 199–200.
Hay, Secretary John, 18.
Hay-Bunau-Varilla treaty, 28, 97, 111.
Hay-Herran treaty, 19.
Hay-Pauncefote treaty, 142, 276, 279.
Hays, President Rutherford B., 275.
Herran, Dr. Thomas, 19.
Hise, Elijah, 273.
Honduras, 169, 268, 273.
Honduras Bay, 163.
Hospitals and sanitariums, 118, 121–122.
Huertas, General, 25.
Hydraulic fill, the, 55.

Incas, 93, 171, 177, 236.
India, 1.
Indians, 33, 149, 164, 170–172, 179, 187, 202–203, 216–217, 226–228, 236–240, 244–249, 269.
    Chibcha Indians, 236.
    Maroon Indians, 202–203, 227.
    Mosquito Indians, 269.
    San Blas Indians, 33, 228, 236, 239–240.
International Scientific Congress, The, 7, 8.

Iron Castle, 191, 195, 206.
Isthmian Canal Commission:
    Departments: of Civil Administration, 99, 112, 132–149, 153; (Divisions: Posts, Customs and Revenues, 134–138; of Police and Prisons, 133–135, 138–141; of Fire Protection, 133–135, 141–142; of Public Works, 112, 135, 142–143; Steam Vessel Inspection Service, 135, 143; of Schools, 135, 145–149; Treasurer, 135, 143; Auditor, 135, 143; Judicial Branch, 136, 143–144); of Construction and Engineering, 30–90, 99, 107, 109, 153, 155; (Divisions: Atlantic, 37–38, 66, 99, 155; Central or Culebra, 85, 99, 155; Pacific, 99, 155; River Hydraulics, Meteorology and Surveys, 70–71, 155); of Disbursements, 99, 150, 154; of Examination of Accounts, 99, 150, 152–154; General Purchasing Office, 99, 150, 152; of Investigations, 99, 150, 154; of Law, 99, 150–151; Quartermaster's, 38, 99, 101–110, 124; of Sanitation, 72–75, 99, 101, 111–123, 153; of Subsistence, 34, 99, 124–131; (Building and Construction Division, 107).

Isthmian Canal Commission:
  Organization, 30, 97–100, 135.
  Relations with Panama, 135, 150.
Italians, 134, 251.

Jackson, President Andrew, 270.
Jamaica, 163, 207, 210, 220–221, 268–269.
Japan, 160.
Japanese, 134.
Jesuit Missionaries in Panama, 227–228.
Jordan, David Starr, 97.
Junta, The revolutionary, of Panama, 22, 25.

La Boca (Balboa), 77, 178.
Las Cascadas, 77.
Leper colony, 122–123.
Le Prince, Mr., 117.
Lidgerwood cars, 86.
Limon Bay, 7, 34, 43, 191, 240, 260.
Lincoln, President Abraham, 275.
Lion Hill, 261.
Living arrangements, 37, 102–107, 116, 133.
Lorenzo, Mount, 33, 211.
Los Santos, Province of, 27.
Louis Philippe, 233.

Magellan, Strait of, 206.
Malaria in Canal Zone, 111, 114–118, 121, 259, 261.
Mansvelt (Dutch pirate), 206–207, 211.

Manzanillo Island, 33, 167, 259–260.
Manzanillo Point, 170.
Markets, Public, 143.
Maroon Indians, 202–203, 227.
Matachin, 77–78.
Mexico, 2, 179, 235–236, 258.
Mindi, 38, 41.
Miraflores Lake, 44, 89.
Miraflores Locks, 44.
Monroe Doctrine, 275.
Morales (explorer), 179.
Morgan, Henry, 4, 180, 196, 205–222.
"Morgan's Bridge," 183.
Mosquito Coast, 163, 269, 274.
Mosquito Indians, 269.
Mosquitoes (campaign against), 75–76, 114–118.
Mount Ancon, 90.
Mount Hope Cemetery, 38.
Mount Hope storehouse, 38, 108.

Naos Island, 47.
Napoleon III, of France, 233, 234.
National Geographic Magazine, 43.
Navy Bay (Limon Bay), 260.
Negotiations of the United States:
  With Colombia, 17–20, 258–259, 262–263; with England, 269, 273–276; with France, 17–19, 264, 267; with Nicaragua, 273; with

Panama, 22–26, 28–29, 97, 131, 135–137, 142, 268.
Negroes, 251.
Nelson, Lord Horatio, 232.
New Edinburg, 231.
New Granada, 19, 270.
New Granada, Treaty with, 258–259, 263, 270, 274.
New Orleans, 125, 152.
New Panama Canal Company, The, 14, 264.
"New Route to India," 159, 160, 166–167, 279–280.
New York, 30, 125, 152.
Nicaragua, 3, 17–18, 28, 206, 232–233, 268, 273, 275.
Night of Horror, 20.
Niña, The, 235.
Niqueza (explorer), 169–171, 189.
Nombre de Dios, 170, 184–195, 200–201, 203–204, 206, 227.

Obaldia, Governor José, 26.
Ojeda, Alfonzo de, 165, 169–170.
Old Panama, 180, 183–184, 190, 195, 201, 206–207, 211–212, 215–221.
Oregon, The, 275–276.

Pacific Ocean, 2, 44, 77, 93, 222.
  Discovery of, 1, 168, 172–178, 235.
Palo Seco, 122.
Panama, Bay of, 7, 175–176, 225.

Panama, Bishop of, 10.
Panama City, 20, 25–26, 28, 90, 111–112, 121, 134, 142, 175, 180, 222–225, 245, 250, 252, 260–261. *See also* Old Panama.
Panama, Isthmus of, 1, 4, 18, 160–166, 169–178; as possible site of canal, 3, 17, 228, 232, 252.
Panama, Province of, 27.
Panama Railroad:
  Commissary Department of, 34, 66, 124.
  Employees of, 43, 102, 138, 141.
  History of, 4, 9, 20, 25–26, 28, 98–100, 258–267, 270.
  Relation to I. C. C., 98, 125, 150.
Panama, Republic of:
  History of, 17–29.
    Negotiations with the United States, 22–26, 28–29, 97, 131, 135–137, 142, 268.
    Relations with Colombia, 19–26.
    Revolution, 17–29; Declaration of Independence, 21–22, 26, 164; government, 26–27; politics, 27, 246; flag, 26, 28.
  Inhabitants of, 134, 234–239, 244–251, 256–257.
  Natural and geographical features, 62, 65, 69, 191, 192, 235, 243–244.

Panama, Republic of :
    Religion of, 27, 246, 249.
Paraiso, 89.
Paris, 7.
Parker (explorer), 196.
Patterson, William, 228–232.
Pearl Islands, 176, 179.
Pedrarias (Pedro Arias de Avila), 176–178, 180, 231.
Pedro Miguel (city), 44, 71, 81–82.
Pedro Miguel Locks, 44.
Peru, 4, 170, 177, 179, 190, 201, 206, 220–222, 235–236.
Philip II, of Spain, 3.
Pinzon (explorer), 235.
Pizarro, Francisco, 93, 170–171, 177–179, 235.
Polo, Marco, 160.
Porto Bello, 104, 164–166, 168, 184, 188, 190–195, 204, 206–210, 219, 221–222, 227, 260.
Protocol, Preliminary, with Colombia, 18.
Public Buildings, 34, 38, 66, 101, 104, 107, 124, 132, 138.
Public Lands, 136.
Puerte del Principe, 207.
Puerto Escoces, 231.

Quarantine, 34, 90.

Rainfall, Statistics regarding, 70–71.
Reports, 101, 128, 150, 153.
Revenues, 136–137, 142–143, 145.
Ringrose (explorer), 196, 225.

Roads in Canal Zone, 137–138, 143.
Robinson, Tracy, 10, 260.
Rolfe, John, 171.
Roosevelt, Theodore, 134.
Roosevelt Avenue, Cristobal, 34, 166.
Rousseau, Commissioner H. H., 14, 61.
Royal Road, The, 179–195, 201, 206, 260.

Saavedra Ceron, Alvaro de, 3.
St. Anastasius, Cathedral of, 183.
St. Andrews, 231.
St. Michael, 175.
San Blas Indians, 33, 228, 236, 239–240.
San Blas Islands, 222.
San Francisco, 125, 152, 276.
San Lorenzo, Fort, 184–188, 211–216, 220–221.
San Miguel, Gulf of, 175–177, 226.
San Pablo, 76, 82.
San Sebastian, 170–171.
Santa Katalina, 206–207, 211, 215.
Santa Maria, 222.
Santa Maria del Antigua, 171–172, 176–177.
Santa Maria, The, 235.
Santo Domingo, 30, 169, 196.
Scandinavians, 134.
Schools in Canal Zone, 132–133, 135, 137, 145–149, 151.
Scotchmen, 134.

Scotland, 231.
"Scrapping" of French Material, 76, 101, 109.
Secretary of the Isthmian Canal Commission, 42, 99, 154.
Seward, Secretary William H., 274.
Sharp (explorer), 196, 222, 226.
Smallpox, 111, 121.
Social Functions, 104, 132, 250–255.
Society of Commercial Geography, 7.
Sosa Hill, 90.
South America, 184, 225.
"South Sea" (Pacific Ocean), 1, 93, 172, 176–178.
Spain:
  Explorations under, 1–4, 159–178, 234–235.
  Interest in canal project, 2–3, 268–269, 280.
  Relations with Colombia, 19.
  Spanish people in Panama, 134, 151, 179–180, 196–201, 206, 208–232, 235–239, 249–251.
Spooner Bill, 17, 264.
Squier, E. G., 273.
Statistics, 16, 42–47, 121, 127–128, 136, 256–257.
Stephens, John L., 259, 263.
Strait, Belief in existence of, 1, 2, 160, 165, 234.
Suez Canal, 7, 9, 13, 47.
Superintendent of Schools, 122.

Supplies, 38, 101–102, 107–109, 124–131.
Syrians, 134, 137.

Tabernilla, 70.
Taboga, 122, 219, 225, 246.
Taft, William H., 267.
Taft Agreement, The, 136.
Tehuantepec, Isthmus of, 3, 179.
Tetu, Captain, 203–204.
Thatcher, Maurice H., 135.
Tides, Ocean, 44.
Tiger Island, 273–274.
Tivoli Hotel, 90, 93, 250, 252.
Toro Point, 33, 47.
Tortuga, Isle of, 210.
Toscanelli's map, 160.
Totten, Colonel G. M., 259.
Track-shifting machines, 72.
Trafalgar, 232.
Treasurer of the Canal Zone, 135, 143.
Treaties:
  Clayton-Bulwer, 273–276.
  Hay-Bunau-Varilla, 28, 97, 111.
  Hay-Herran, 19.
  Hay-Pauncefote, 142, 276, 279.
  With New Granada, 258–259, 263, 270, 274.
Trinidad, 200.
Tuberculosis in Canal Zone, 121.
Turin, Italy, 166.
Turks, 134.
Tuyra River, 228.

INDEX

Typhoid fever in Canal Zone, 121.

Universal Interoceanic Company, The, 8, 9, 13.

Vela, Cape de la, 169.
Venezuela, 165, 169.
Venta Cruz (Cruces), 184.
Vera Cruz, 199, 211.
Veraguas, Province of, 27, 164.
Vespucci, Amerigo, 234.
Victuals, Isle of, 164.
Von Humboldt, Baron, 232.

Wafer, Lionel, 196, 225–226, 228.
Washington Hotel, Colon, 262.
Watling's Island, 30.
West Indians, 78, 134, 138, 149, 151, 196, 251.
West Indies, 1, 196, 210.
Wilson, Major Eugene T., 125.
Wyse, Lieutenant, 175.

Yaviza, 228.
Yellow Fever in Canal Zone, 111, 114–117, 121.
Yucatan, 235–236.
Y. M. C. A., 66, 104, 252, 255.

Related Titles from Westphalia Press

The Limits of Moderation: Jimmy Carter and the Ironies of American Liberalism

The Limits of Moderation: Jimmy Carter and the Ironies of American Liberalism is not a finished product. And yet, even in this unfinished stage, this book is a close and careful history of a short yet transformative period in American political history, when big changes were afoot.

The Zelensky Method
by Grant Farred

Locating Russian's war within a global context, The Zelensky Method is unsparing in its critique of those nations, who have refused to condemn Russia's invasion and are doing everything they can to prevent economic sanctions from being imposed on the Kremlin.

Sinking into the Honey Trap: The Case of the Israeli-Palestinian Conflict
by Daniel Bar-Tal, Barbara Doron, Translator

Sinking into the Honey Trap by Daniel Bar-Tal discusses how politics led Israel to advancing the occupation, and of the deterioration of democracy and morality that accelerates the growth of an authoritarian regime with nationalism and religiosity.

Essay on The Mysteries and the True Object of The Brotherhood of Freemasons
by Jason Williams

The third edition of Essai sur les mystères discusses Freemasonry's role as a society of symbolic philosophers who cultivate their minds, practice virtues, and engage in charity, and underscores the importance of brotherhood, morality, and goodwill.

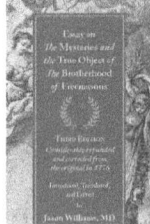

Bunker Diplomacy: An Arab-American in the U.S. Foreign Service
by Nabeel Khoury

After twenty-five years in the Foreign Service, Dr. Nabeel A. Khoury retired from the U.S. Department of State in 2013 with the rank of Minister Counselor. In his last overseas posting, Khoury served as deputy chief of mission at the U.S. embassy in Yemen (2004-2007).

Managing Challenges for the Flint Water Crisis
Edited by Toyna E. Thornton, Andrew D. Williams, Katherine M. Simon, Jennifer F. Sklarew

This edited volume examines several public management and intergovernmental failures, with particular attention on social, political, and financial impacts. Understanding disaster meaning, even causality, is essential to the problem-solving process.

User-Centric Design
by Dr. Diane Stottlemyer

User-centric strategy can improve by using tools to manage performance using specific techniques. User-centric design is based on and centered around the users. They are an essential part of the design process and should have a say in what they want and need from the application based on behavior and performance.

Masonic Myths and Legends
by Pierre Mollier

Freemasonry is one of the few organizations whose teaching method is still based on symbols. It presents these symbols by inserting them into legends that are told to its members in initiation ceremonies. But its history itself has also given rise to a whole mythology.

Abortion and Informed Common Sense
by Max J. Skidmore

The controversy over a woman's "right to choose," as opposed to the numerous "rights" that abortion opponents decide should be assumed to exist for "unborn children," has always struck me as incomplete. Two missing elements of the argument seems obvious, yet they remain almost completely overlooked.

The Athenian Year Primer: Attic Time-Reckoning and the Julian Calendar
by Christopher Planeaux

The ability to translate ancient Athenian calendar references into precise Julian-Gregorian dates will not only assist Ancient Historians and Classicists to date numerous historical events with much greater accuracy but also aid epigraphists in the restorations of numerous Attic inscriptions.

Siddhartha: Life of the Buddha
by David L. Phillips,
contributions by Venerable Sitagu Sayadaw

Siddhartha: Life of the Buddha is an illustrated story for adults and children about the Buddha's birth, enlightenment and work for social justice. It includes illustrations from Pagan, Burma which are provided by Rev. Sitagu Sayadaw.

Growing Inequality: Bridging Complex Systems, Population Health, and Health Disparities
Editors: George A. Kaplan, Ana V. Diez Roux, Carl P. Simon, and Sandro Galea

Why is America's health is poorer than the health of other wealthy countries and why health inequities persist despite our efforts? In this book, researchers report on groundbreaking insights to simulate how these determinants come together to produce levels of population health and disparities and test new solutions.

Issues in Maritime Cyber Security
Edited by Dr. Joe DiRenzo III, Dr. Nicole K. Drumhiller, and Dr. Fred S. Roberts

The complexity of making MTS safe from cyber attack is daunting and the need for all stakeholders in both government (at all levels) and private industry to be involved in cyber security is more significant than ever as the use of the MTS continues to grow.

Female Emancipation and Masonic Membership: An Essential Collection
By Guillermo De Los Reyes Heredia

Female Emancipation and Masonic Membership: An Essential Combination is a collection of essays on Freemasonry and gender that promotes a transatlantic discussion of the study of the history of women and Freemasonry and their contribution in different countries.

Anti-Poverty Measures in America: Scientism and Other Obstacles
Editors, Max J. Skidmore and Biko Koenig

Anti-Poverty Measures in America brings together a remarkable collection of essays dealing with the inhibiting effects of scientism, an over-dependence on scientific methodology that is prevalent in the social sciences, and other obstacles to anti-poverty legislation.

Geopolitics of Outer Space: Global Security and Development
by Ilayda Aydin

A desire for increased security and rapid development is driving nation-states to engage in an intensifying competition for the unique assets of space. This book analyses the Chinese-American space discourse from the lenses of international relations theory, history and political psychology to explore these questions.

Contests of Initiative: Countering China's Gray Zone Strategy in the East and South China Seas
by Dr. Raymond Kuo

China is engaged in a widespread assertion of sovereignty in the South and East China Seas. It employs a "gray zone" strategy: using coercive but sub-conventional military power to drive off challengers and prevent escalation, while simultaneously seizing territory and asserting maritime control.

Discourse of the Inquisitive
Editors: Jaclyn Maria Fowler and Bjorn Mercer

Good communication skills are necessary for articulating learning, especially in online classrooms. It is often through writing that learners demonstrate their ability to analyze and synthesize the new concepts presented in the classroom.

westphaliapress.org

Policy Studies Organization

The Policy Studies Organization (PSO) is a publisher of academic journals and book series, sponsor of conferences, and producer of programs.

Policy Studies Organization publishes dozens of journals on a range of topics, such as European Policy Analysis, Journal of Elder Studies, Indian Politics & Polity, Journal of Critical Infrastructure Policy, and Popular Culture Review.

Additionally, Policy Studies Organization hosts numerous conferences. These conferences include the Middle East Dialogue, Space Education and Strategic Applications Conference, International Criminology Conference, Dupont Summit on Science, Technology and Environmental Policy, World Conference on Fraternalism, Freemasonry and History, and the Internet Policy & Politics Conference.

For more information on these projects, access videos of past events, and upcoming events, please visit us at:

www.ipsonet.org

www.ingramcontent.com/pod-product-compliance
Lightning Source LLC
Chambersburg PA
CBHW051528020426
42333CB00016B/1826